WILD GREEN ORANGES

AN AUTOBIOGRAPHICAL NOVEL

by Bob Baldock

The Clapton Press

Wild Green Oranges © 2021 Bob Baldock

All rights reserved.

This edition published by:

The Clapton Press Limited
38 Thistlewaite Road
London E5 0QQ

ISBN: 978-1-9996543-10-7

Cover design: Bob Baldock & Ivana Nohel

CONTENTS

for Kathleen

1

Christmas season, 1956: A small college town in Ohio

When the first ghostly haze of dawn began drifting in through the bare trees on the hilltop, I turned my back on the fire's waning warmth and, squatting down in the snow, rolled the sleeping bag into a tight bundle and stuffed it into my gym bag. With the flames extinguished, I felt even more alone. She was gone. There wasn't much beyond her death. I kicked loose snow over the fading coals and grabbed the gym bag and started back to town. The only difficult part of the descent was a steep stretch over snow-glazed shale. This led to a birch copse stretching down to an abandoned mud road that led to exhausted strip-mines further back in the hills. I went in the other direction, toward town, a distance of five or six miles, taking my time, stamping ice puddles along the way, finally reaching the deserted campus. All the buildings seemed empty, as did the sorority and fraternity houses.

By the time I got to the library my teeth ached with cold. The massive wooden doors were locked, so I continued on across campus to the town. Coal ash had been scattered over the sidewalks to allow traction over the ice. A few people were cautiously picking their way along the main street. Except for a county sheriff checking parking meters, they all looked like townspeople—strip miners and their families. I'd been told they resented the college, yet I felt better seeing them. Most of the folks seemed less beaten down than usual, probably because the students were gone for the holidays. The bars and pizza parlors were closed. I didn't see a single sports car, just pick-up trucks and unwashed family sedans. I cut across a used car lot and walked uphill to the cheap rooming house where I was living.

On the ground floor was a meager grocery store run by my landlady. I pulled the door open, ringing a cowbell above it.

"Here's the other one now," Mrs Gussker said. She was behind the counter, waiting on an athletic young guy in a black wool poncho. His head was entirely bald.

"The other one?" I said.

"I was just telling Griffin here that you two are most likely the only students left in town. You know each other?"

"Not yet," he said.

"Don''t believe any of his jive, Paul," said Mrs Gussker. She was habitually gruff, yet clearly fond of this guy.

"Get me a quart of your watered-down cider, Mrs Gus" he said, before turning back to me. "Just call me Griffin."

"I'm Paul," I said, "Paul Bell."

He nodded and caught my hand in a powerful grip.

Mrs Gussker returned with the cider. He wedged it into a cardboard carton filled with groceries. The shop stocked a number of unpackaged products from local farms—fresh cider, apple sauce, mushrooms, unwrapped cheeses, even fresh vegetables in season. While Mrs Gussker acknowledged having been here for decades, her accent had me assuming she'd come from Eastern Europe.

"Debtors should speak well of others," she muttered, writing something in an account book.

I wandered down an aisle to find a few items to get me through the rest of the vacation. All I really wanted was sleep. When I returned to the counter, Griffin had his carton balanced on one shoulder. He hesitated at the door.

"Hey, Bell, see you around," he said. "Come out to my place."

"Don't heat the whole outdoors," Mrs Gussker shouted, waving him out.

"*Feliz navidad*, Mrs Gus." He blew her a kiss with his free hand.

The cowbell tinkled sharply before the door slammed shut, leaving Mrs Gussker and me looking quizzically at each other.

"I'll be closed tomorrow and Christmas Day," she said. "Best get everything you're gonna need right now."

I found a loaf of wheat bread and three yellow apples, then stood waiting while she consulted the account book.

"I don't believe he's paid me for one solitary thing this entire month," she murmured.

"Is he really a student?" I asked.

"He's a weirdo." She dropped the account book into a tin box. "He's a student all right. There's not much more I know about him."

"Do you know what's wrong with him?"

She frowned blankly at me.

"Is it cancer?" I said bluntly.

"What on earth makes you ask that?"

"What made his hair fall out?"

"What makes you think he didn't just shave his head?"

"Why would anyone shave their head?"

"You'll have to ask him."

"Any idea why he's here over the holidays?"

"He's been here every vacation for three years now. He's all right, I expect, just a little wild."

"Wild?"

"Living in the woods and all. Like a gypsy. He's close-mouthed about himself. Most likely his folks kicked him out."

She dropped my groceries into a paper sack and bent down to rummage behind the *True Love* magazines and

9

knitting patterns she kept under the counter. She brought up several discolored pictures neatly scissored from the college paper. Griffin was easily recognizable. In the first, wearing black tights and a fierce expression, he was suspended in mid-air in a dancer's leap above the caption "Sophomore R. Griffin to be male dance lead in Annual College Carnival."

The second photo showed him staring defiantly from among a group of some twenty seated men, all African-American except him. The caption had been torn off.

"Dandy, isn't it?" Mrs Gussker shook her head. "Just look at him sitting there all self-righteous. Lord God."

"What is this?" I asked.

"Young fool wanted to show off, to prove something or other. He joined the colored fraternity. Likely some white fraternity would have taken him, but he had to prove something."

"You know where he's living?"

"The very first time you came in here asking about a room I suspected you two might take to each other. Like hawks to hares."

"I'm just curious."

She frowned wearily. "On the other side of campus, beyond the football fields, way up in the woods there somewhere. So he says."

* * *

Around noon the next day I threw off two Army blankets and the old rug covering my bed and crossed the bare floor to the sink. The water was icy and rust-colored. I let it run while I pulled on my shoes, still sodden. I held my head under the faucet for a moment before prying the cold soap from the porcelain. I washed my face, brushed my teeth, then made a peanut butter sandwich. I ate it sitting on the bed, washing it down with cider, wondering what to do next. I decided to go to the drugstore and see if they had any new paperbacks.

The air was fresh outside, sharp, only slightly colder than my room. The low sky seemed ready to drop a world of snow. Three boys were playing basketball in the street under a beat-up metal sign serving as a backboard. It was too cold for the ball to bounce so they just fired passes back and forth. On the main street there were more people than usual. Above the clicking of rusted tire-chains I could hear the blare of a loudspeaker rasping out carols from the record shop.

I was almost at the drugstore when I recognized Griffin's distinctive head. He was standing under the unlit marquee of the town's only movie theater, studying posters of coming attractions. He was wearing a black sweatshirt and black slacks with a bright red scarf.

"I've seen it," I called out to him. "Save your money."

"Hey," he said, spinning around. "How's it going?"

"Not bad," I replied, "How about you?

"Where you heading?"

I shrugged.

"Walk with me back to my place. Come on."

I hesitated but matched his fast pace, as we dodged people coming toward us on the sidewalk.

"You live above Mrs Gus," he said.

"That's right."

"I know those rooms, bleak, no heat."

"I like it."

"Sheer stoicism." He smiled at me with what seemed like real friendliness. His gloved hand slapped each parking meter we passed.

"Mrs Gussker told me you've been here quite a while," I said.

"This is my fourth year. I graduate this spring. You're a sophomore?"

"That's right."

"Just what else did she say?"

"She follows you avidly, you know. She showed me some clippings."

"You're kidding!" he said, clearly pleased. "She kept clippings? I've got a stupendous bill with her. She really doesn't want me to pay it. She's a genuine fairy godmother, Mrs Gus. What a sweetheart. Which clippings did she show you?"

"Just a couple," I said.

He looked dismayed. I broke out laughing, and so did he, before he suddenly jabbed my shoulder and broke away running. After a few steps he hurled himself into the air, red scarf rippling out behind him as he flipped head over feet through three flying cartwheels along the sidewalk. When I caught up to him, he was brushing snow off his sweatshirt and grinning with satisfaction.

We walked on together, neither of us saying much. The snow creaked beneath our boots as we left the campus and started across the athletic fields toward the hills. A cold wind laced with fresh bits of snow blew past us in gusts that rattled the metal signs on the grandstand and caused old score cards to flutter along the empty tiers of seats.

"You actually *do* live in the woods," I said. "How do you manage it?"

"You'll see." He led me to the far side of the fields and then on through birch woods scattered with clusters of evergreens. Our pace was slowed by brambles and vines. He walked in front, ducking under low branches until we came to a barbed wire fence. At that point he stopped, holding the top strand of wire as high as it would lift. I bent down and awkwardly got myself through one leg at a time, then turned around to hold up the wire for him. But he dropped a hand on a fencepost and vaulted smoothly over. I hurried after him, feeling a little foolish. I followed him down an incline that led to a small clearing. At the far end of it was a tent enlarged by a lean-to built next to it and made of birch branches covered with canvas and topped with pine boughs.

"Beautiful!" I exclaimed, genuinely delighted. "It's great! Is it rain-proof?"

He nodded, strode across the clearing and ducked into the structure. This austere set-up was precisely the way I would have lived if the idea had ever occurred to me. It struck me as being . . . sufficient, exactly sufficient. On one side of the clearing he'd rigged a small stone fireplace with a metal grill. Beside it was a sizable pile of twigs and pinecones.

"What do you do for water?" I called out.

"Come on in," he shouted. "There's a spring over there by the Christmas tree."

I looked around and saw a shaggy blue spruce even before I heard the sound of water trickling over stones. He had fashioned a little pool near the base of the tree by digging out rocks and removing roots. Dead leaves were swirling slowly on the surface. I found a long stick and started flicking them out. Suddenly I was struck by an overwhelming yearning for her, for Anna, a hunger for her just to be here, to see this little clearing under the bone-white sky, for her to meet my new friend, to be having this experience with me.

"You still here?" Griffin called.

"Yeah, right here."

I forced back a welling of tears, blinking rapidly.

"Get in here before you freeze."

I tossed the stick away and slipped into the tent. Inside were two cots—one covered with books, the other with a Boy Scout sleeping bag. Griffin sat on it, fiddling impatiently with an old heater.

"This is terrific," I said. "The college lets you live out here?"

"You like it?" he said vaguely, wiring the heater to a car battery on the floor.

I dropped onto the empty cot. He didn't answer me. Quite a collection of things was stashed on makeshift orange-crate shelving—a typewriter, camera, binoculars, two kerosene lanterns, a .22 rifle, a box of rubbers, and a couple dozen books, some of them in Spanish. More crates were shoved under the cots.

"I've got some red wine here, Côtes du Rhône, I think. You want yours hot or cold?"

"Wine? You can heat it?"

"It's best that way, this kind of weather."

"Okay," I said. "You know, I saw those clippings Mrs Gussker had, but there were only three of them."

"She's missing a lot." He poured wine into a speckled enamel cup and set it on top of the heater. "Mrs Gus told me about you," he went on. "You don't live in a dorm."

I started to say something but he went on, "Sophomore year I was in a dorm. A bunch of wholesome all-American boys started screwing with me. I was studying dance, performance dance, and they decided it was their business. If you're not in the herd, it stampedes you. I was doing a lot of yoga exercises, dancing. A few guys started playing stupid tricks. Peeing in my shaving lotion, things of that caliber. One night I caught three of them messing with my stuff.

"And?" I said.

"I hurt them. I'm against violence but I punished all three of them. Here, drink this while it's hot."

He handed me a metal cup, warm with the fragrant wine. I blew off the steam, swirled the pink foam, and took a tentative swallow. It wasn't bad, although the sour heat made me cough.

"You *punished* them?" I said. "They put you on probation?"

"Nah. I told them I'd never go back to that dorm, or any other dorm. Trouble was, they had a rule you couldn't live outside a dorm or a fraternity house unless you were

14

married or twenty-one. I was twenty, so I joined a fraternity. Mrs Gus has a clipping about it."

"I saw it."

"I didn't fit in. The frat guys were okay, but doing stuff as a collective, that got odd." He tilted the cup to his mouth and gulped the wine straight down without stopping to breathe. I watched the sinewy muscles of his throat until he stopped and set the cup on an orange crate. Then he offered me one of those little black cigarettes with the gold tip.

"I don't smoke."

"Neither do I," he said. "It's just slow suicide. Try one anyway. One won't harm you. A girl gave me these. They're Russian, Balkan Sobranie. Try one. That strong flavor is *Latakia*, a Turkish tobacco."

"They're wasted on me," I said, nevertheless picking one out of the tin box and holding it while he scratched a match on the battery. He lit mine before putting the match to his own. I started coughing again.

"Where'd you get that scar on your wrist?" he asked. "You self-destructive?"

"A steel mill," I said. "I worked in one."

"Mrs Gus said you have a scholarship."

"It only pays tuition. One of those athletic deals. Basketball."

He looked at me in a way suggesting he was doing some reappraising.

"Really? You're a jock?"

"Just basketball."

"And you worked in a steel mill?"

"For two years. Pipe-glazing. Dangerous stuff, but the guys I worked with—older, family guys from the south, mostly black guys—they were terrific. They looked out for me."

"So what are you studying?" he asked.

"Liberal Arts. I'd like to learn how to write."

"An aspiring novelist."

"More like an aspiring journalist."

"Watch out—journalism can be pretty subversive around here. Do one thing differently in this cow-plop of a college and right away reactionary jerks start hassling you. I'm a vegetarian, so naturally I'm not normal. I like to be alone with a woman instead of pawing her at some prom. I dance, so naturally I'm a homo."

"Get many rabbits?" I asked him.

"Rabbits?"

"You hunt, don't you?"

"I hate hunting and fishing."

"So what's with the .22?"

"Ah, that," he said bemusedly. "A gift. But what about you?"

"With all these things happening to you," I said, "how is it you're still in school?"

"It's hard to get thrown out of here," he laughed. "I want this degree. I've completed the requirements, except for two papers. I arrived just before military training became compulsory. Otherwise I'd never have lasted. I hate the Army—all those morons marching around, acting all *macho*—"

"I'm in ROTC," I interrupted. "Army ROTC," I stood up. "It was mandatory." He didn't seem to register what I was saying.

"One night," he went on, "a bunch of guys, probably junior officers, ROTC types, came prowling around here with flashlights. I heard them coming, a bunch of loudmouths. I hid in the woods and watched them throw my stuff around, about eight of them. They tore up some of my books."

"Really?"

"You probably heard about it, you being a proud member of ROTC."

16

I took a few deep breaths at the flap of the tent. It was twilight. Snowflakes were drifting down in the clearing, and the air smelled as if there were many more on their way.

"No." I shook my head. "I never heard anything. Did they destroy a lot of books?"

"Enough. But it's my final year. They don't assign much reading."

"What's your major?"

"I started with drama, then added dance. Each of the last two summers I worked out with José Limón's dance troupe in Connecticut."

"I didn't know dance could be a major."

"Limón's troupe did a performance here my first year," he said. "It really made me want to dance. Ever tried it?" He ignored my expression. "You're tall, but one of their lead dancers, Lucas Hoving, is six feet eight, lithe as a leopard."

"That what has you in such good shape?"

"It helps. First year here I worked out at the gym, lifted weights, special diet, the whole routine. In Puerto Rico there was no way to seriously work out, not where we lived."

"You're from Puerto Rico?"

"My mother is. My father was stationed there when I was born. Listen, I don't know about you, but I'm starving and I've got a whole lot of stuff here from Mrs Gus."

"I could eat." I was comfortable just sitting there listening. I felt an interest in him I hadn't felt in anyone or anything for some time. He was strange, but I liked him. There was something about him I felt myself responding to, something under the surface. I felt a sort of instinctive accord I'd never felt before, except with Anna, and she was gone. As he talked, the light faded against the canvas of the tent. In the growing darkness the heater on the floor between us glowed a richer red, giving warmth to the

17

smokiness. I watched Griffin's face gradually take on a ruddy cast as he leaned forward over the heater, puffing occasionally on one of the cigarettes, from time to time poking me on the knee for emphasis.

"That .22 work?" I asked.

"Probably," he said brusquely. "The girl that gave it to me was one I was going with during that lynch mob visit. She thought I needed it. I doubt I'd ever actually use the thing. Probably I'll hock it, but listen, there's wood behind the tent. Could you get some? I'm going to take a crap."

I carried an armload of small logs over to the fireplace and started a little blaze. They burned swiftly, throwing up sparks and crackling orange flames as the snowflakes came down more and more thickly. Griffin returned carrying a carton that held two big cans of baked beans. We cooked both cans in an iron pot over the fire, stirring in cheddar cheese and tomato catsup and pepper until the beans were simmering, then bubbling. Their fragrance of molasses and pork and tomatoes was especially pungent in that clearing with the snow swirling. We ate standing at the fireplace taking the beans sizzling straight from the pot with long wooden spoons, eating too avidly to talk. Wood smoke mingled with the other flavors.

"This is terrific," I said, and it did taste great to me, eaten just like that, standing in the snow, pausing only to take turns drinking icy spring water from his tin cup.

"I think this is the best meal I've had in a long time, Griffin."

"Glad you're okay with it."

When I finally set my spoon down, I watched him scrape the last few burned morsels from the bottom of the pot.

"Coffee pot in the tent," he said. "Get it and I'll make coffee. I love coffee."

I started for the tent.

"There's honey, too," he called after me. He sounded more upbeat than he'd been all afternoon, but when I got back with the various things he was staring moodily into the fire.

"Let's get the coffee going," he said abruptly. "Just fill the pot at the spring over there."

I did as directed while Griffin poured out a bit of water and added the coffee beans. He'd crushed them with a flat stone on the fireplace. As soon as the thick liquid began boiling he sloshed it into the tin cup and added a splash of milk and a gob of comb honey.

"You're not very talkative, Paul," he said.

I shrugged, controlling an impulse to blurt out my grief, to let him know. Then his gaze returned to the fire. There was only the hushed sound of snow drifting through the trees. That and the steady crackling of the fire.

"Well, guess I'd better be getting back to town," I finally said.

"Think you can find your way? The woods will be dark."

"I think so, yeah. Thanks for everything. Sorry I'm so quiet."

He glanced at me and nodded thoughtfully.

"You happen to be in town the next few days," I said, "you might drop by my room, have a cup of coffee. I mean, if you feel like it."

"Maybe I'll do that," he said.

Leaving him standing beside the fire I walked rapidly across the clearing and into the trees. Like he said, it was dark among them, despite a blue glow rising from patches of old snow. Once or twice I stumbled over roots or unseen boulders, but gradually my eyes became accustomed to the dark. By the time I reached the barbed wire fence I knew where I was. It occurred to me I was feeling somewhat better.

* * *

19

On Christmas Day, from early morning on, I studied, with a blanket and rug draped over my shoulders. Late afternoon I gave it up and left the room to wander around town. A stillness nearly arctic hung over everything. For an hour or so I drifted around, watching lights blink on like golden squares of inaccessible warmth in the windows of the old, worn houses. Many of these townspeople were out of work. It was moving to see a few of them making an effort at celebration. Here and there wreaths or strings of bright plastic bells hung on front doors. Through one window I could see a piano decked with greeting cards. Passing a particularly decrepit house, I caught a glimpse of an old man, white-haired and terribly bent. He was lighting a candle in the front window.

Just as I was about to return to my room, I saw something that stabbed at the pit of my stomach. With a glittering tree behind him, a pale little boy was pressing his nose against the cold pane of a smudged window, slowly swinging his head from side to side. His eyes had a dull look as he stared out, waiting for Santa or merely watching twilight darken into an icy purple. I halted in front of his house and watched him for a long while, until finally across the stillness of his front yard our eyes met, and I waved. He didn't move. He stared at me with absolutely no expression. Long minutes must have passed before he turned and disappeared into the house. For one bewildering split-second it seemed to me that a voice had called him from the kitchen, my mother's voice.

* * *

The packet of letters smelled distinctly of the subtle lilac fragrance she often wore, one I had always liked. She thought it was from a delicate flower that grew high in the Austrian Alps, where she had lived as a child. I removed the rubber band and inhaled deeply, then stopped myself. I knew I shouldn't look at the letters again. There were less than a dozen, describing how she missed me, but appreciated my going to college, getting out in the world. For a few minutes I stood in the center of the room, over and over again pulling the string that turned on and off the bare light bulb suspended from the ceiling. Then, impulsively, I tossed the packet into the sink, struck a wooden match with my thumb, and started burning the letters and envelopes one at a time, watching them curl up in flames and turn to ash. The tap water, rusty as usual, washed away the ashes. The smoke burned my eyes, so I wrenched opened the window above the sink, then just stood there, dully watching the smoke drift out and up into the night sky. Many long minutes must have passed before I became conscious of banging on my front door .

"*Hola,* open up!" Griffin was shouting. I unlocked the door and he landed a friendly punch on my shoulder as he pushed past me into the room.

"Merry Christmas, Mister Paul Bell," he said excitedly. "Had supper yet?"

He started to shuffle through the pile of books on my kitchen table. "Who's this Herman Hesse? Did you burn your supper?"

My eyes were stinging. I took a deep breath and let it out slowly before looking up and holding his gaze.

"I've been wanting to tell you something," I said. "My sweetheart, Anna, is dead, my fiancée, killed. She was hit in the crosswalk by a hit and run driver and she died. She's gone. We were going to be married."

He nodded, holding my eyes with what felt like genuine empathy.

"When did this happen?" he asked quietly.

"Three weeks ago, just after Thanksgiving. Just after I came back here. I should have stayed in Pittsburgh. I should have stayed with her. She'd still be alive."

"You weren't there when it happened?"

"I was here. I should never have left Pittsburgh. Her mother phoned and told me. My father said he was sorry, but he wasn't. Not really. They didn't like her, my folks, although they didn't know her at all. They never wanted to know her. I loved her so much. Anna. I still do."

"Sit down," Griffin urged me.

I hesitated, then slumped onto a kitchen chair.

He put his arm around my shoulders. It was awkward.

"Stop talking," he said, "Just stop. That's enough for now."

He watched me trying to get my breathing under control.

"Let's get out of here," he snapped, snatching my jacket off the bed and tossing it at me. I tugged it on and followed him, clattering down the stairs just behind him. It felt okay being with this guy, jogging along side by side through the empty streets, heading nowhere in particular.

"You read too much," he said. "All those morbid books you have. I'll bet you worry about nuclear war, too. As a student of psychology, a particularly gifted one, I advise you to jettison all those existential books."

"At least I'm not a hermit."

"Sure about that?"

I had no idea where we were going, but we were going there faster and faster. I could feel a physical heaviness beginning to slip away.

"I'm not the one who lives alone in the woods," I said.

"But you're a hermit, Paul Bell, and an introspective goddamn sophomore hermit at that. So just watch your lip."

He jabbed an elbow into my ribs and moved out ahead of me. I quickened my pace. He moved even faster and glanced tauntingly back at me, so I put on more speed and drew alongside him. By then we were both running close to all out.

"Where are we going?" I shouted.

"Who knows?" he yelled, still breathing easily. "Just don't try to outrun me. It's never been done."

Snorting loudly at that, I sprinted beside him through a parking lot and into the middle of the street. Then we were running all out. He stayed beside me past a block of dark shops and then another until I felt a sudden release of new energy, like a second wind but greater in force. I broke away and kept on running, putting every ounce of muscle and energy into the effort, until suddenly I was free and flying along by myself, sucking in great lungfuls of night air and leaving Griffin farther and farther behind as the adrenaline kicked in. He shouted something but the words fell away as I kept on running, feeling I could soar off the face of the earth, racing wildly past the last buildings on campus and out over the open fields, running as I hadn't run since Anna had run beside me with that athletic grace she had.

Finally I skidded forward and fell, hurtling into a hedge before pitching straight on through it and slamming into a deep snowdrift. There I sprawled, gasping for air, feeling the snow burn into the sweat on my face. Trickles of snowmelt ran down under my collar and onto my chest. The fierce coldness of it felt sensationally good. I took a huge bite from a handful of snow and felt it slide burning down my throat, already raw from running. Then Griffin burst into view and threw himself down next to me.

"Would have been here sooner," he gasped, "didn't want to outdo a friend."

I looked at him and found myself laughing. I scooped up a handful of snow and dropped it on his face. He didn't retaliate.

"That's by far the best sound I've heard from you," he said.

"What is?"

"Laughing. You should try it more often. God Almighty, you can run."

"It's the basketball," I said. "I'm in shape."

We lay there in the snow bank, gradually recovering our breath. It struck me he was secretly pleased I'd beaten him. Considering that, I propped myself up on one elbow and looked down at him. He was staring with an odd expression straight up at the opaque black sky.

2

January, 1957

The new year was well under way before I saw Griffin
again. I had said goodbye to my favorite professor and the
basketball coach, and was feeling relieved with the decision
to quit school. Griffin had come by my room several times
but I'd missed him. Now I was determined to find him
before leaving town. An unseasonable thaw was underway.
Slabs of wet snow were sliding down eaves onto the lawns.
The temperature was so mild I had the window in my room
propped wide open so I could feel the breeze and hear the
dripping icicles while I packed. Still unanswered was the
question of where I was going. So far it seemed my
destination would be wherever the first Greyhound bus
was headed. The things I wanted to keep—books, clothes,
my toilet kit—fit into a single suitcase and my gym bag. The
hotplate, a few grocery odds and ends, and half a dozen
paperbacks were in a sack I wanted to leave with Griffin. At
last I popped open a beer can and carried it back and forth
across the room while mulling over my plan once again.

It seemed sound enough, if perturbingly inconclusive.

Leaving my bags on the bed, I started out with the sack
for Griffin's place, dropping into the grocery store just long
enough to pay Mrs Gussker my back rent. Suppertime air
around the strip miners' houses was dark blue and humid,
filled with the sounds of thaw, fragrant with the smells of
cabbage cooking, coal smoke, and garlic. Authentic spring

was still months off, yet in several side yards I could see laundry already hung out to dry. Stores were open late on Friday nights, and the sidewalks were thronged with residents and returned students getting early starts on their weekend. Cars roared along Main Street, only to swing into U-turns and come showboating back. In the pizza parlor and hamburger havens groups of students crowded around pinball machines and jukeboxes. All four blocks of commerce were bright with lights and noise.

The weekend had begun on the campus too. I heard the discordant rhythms of a band tuning up in the gymnasium. Light filled its windows while a spot-lit banner over the entrance proclaimed "The Pleasures of Paris Prom". When I reached the athletic fields, I noticed the snow had mostly vanished, leaving the dead grass soggy. Behind the grandstand, I broke into a sprint and kept it up all the way across the football field, holding the sack like a football, dodging countless invisible tacklers. When I finally made it to Griffin's clearing, I felt a certain relief when I saw his dark silhouette patterned on the canvas.

"Hey, Griffin," I called out. No answer. I called again. At last his voice boomed out, gruff and impatient. "Who is it?"

"It's Bell, Paul Bell."

"Advance," he shouted.

"Good to see you," I exclaimed, ducking into the tent.

"Be with you right away," he said distractedly. Seating myself on one of the cots, I noticed a dark suit laid out neatly on the other one. An assortment of odd liquor bottles was arranged on the crate shelves. I was surprised to see two paperbacks by Herman Hesse. Griffin doused his head in a basin of water and started rubbing away with a clean tee-shirt the frothy traces of shaving cream on the top of his head and along his jaw.

"I'm just here for a minute," I explained. "I brought a few things I thought you might be able to use."

"There's plum brandy in that silver decanter. Try it. Slivovitz or something. Pure vitamin. Drink it straight from the decanter." He finished drying his head and sprinkled on some cologne before swiftly buttoning up a white dress shirt.

"In a hurry," he said. "Got a date with this voluptuous *chica* and I'm running late. Try the brandy. It was a gift."

"I noticed there's a big dance going on at the gym. Pleasures of Paris, right?"

He grunted and hastily began knotting a black silk tie, concentrating on doing a Windsor knot. "We're going away for the weekend. We've even got a car."

"Sounds good. I see you got some Hesse books."

"Someone recommended him. Aren't you even going to taste that?

He stepped into the black suit trousers, zipped them quickly and buckled the belt tight. I poured a tiny amount of the plum brandy into a tin cup. He shrugged on the stylish black jacket.

"Not bad," I said.

"Yeah?" he inquired, posing in front of me, clearly pleased. "By not bad you mean to say sophisticated as hell, irresistibly suave, the cool Latino himself."

He plucked the decanter from my hand and tilted it carefully to his mouth. After gargling a mouthful he set the decanter back among the other bottles and spat into the basin of soapy water.

"What've you got there?" he asked.

"Stuff I thought you could use, like food and a hotplate and—"

"Just leave it on the cot there. Walk me back to the campus. I have to pick up my date at the Delta house."

I put the sack on the cot and stood up. "I was planning on going in the other direction."

"Other direction?" he said, blowing out the lantern and nudging me out of the tent. "You're not going back to town?"

"I thought I'd go up into the hills tonight."

He paused in the clearing with a mildly annoyed air. "Well, let's get together soon then, okay? Sorry I have to run like this. You sure you won't be needing any of those things?"

"You can have them," I said. "I just stopped by to let you know I'm taking off. Leaving school. I just wanted to say goodbye."

I extended my hand. He didn't take it because he didn't see it. He was looking into my eyes with an uncomprehending frown.

"You're kidding," he said.

"Nope."

"You're leaving? Just like that?"

"Just like that."

He hesitated, pushing his fists into his coat pockets and glancing around the clearing.

"Listen," he said, sounding particularly earnest. "Walk me back to the campus and tell me about it. Come on. We can talk on the way."

"I'm pretty much set on going up into the hills."

"All right then. Tell you what. I'll drop by your room Sunday night. I can be there by five. Don't do anything until then."

"I'll be long gone."

"Well, tomorrow then, noon, at your place. I'll spend the night with my date and then see you in the—no, I can't, damn it. Look, tomorrow afternoon. That be okay?"

"The thing is," I said, "I don't want to hang around. I'm all packed. By noon I'll be gone. But I'll write, that's a promise."

He shrugged. "If that's the way you want it," he said resignedly.

I hesitated.

"Okay," he said. "I guess we'll see each other somewhere, sometime."

We shook hands. I wanted to walk back with him but understood his rush to get with his date and didn't want to be in the way.

"Take care of yourself, Griff," I said.

"You do the same, Bell."

I stood there for another moment, watching him move away, then I pivoted and started toward the hills. Just as I was entering the trees I heard his shout.

"Paul, hold on!"

I turned just in time to see him dart into the tent. The branch I'd just pushed away sprang back and slapped hard into my face, but it didn't have anywhere near the impact of Griffin's voice.

"Hold on while I change clothes!" he yelled.

I started to protest, but the words didn't come out, so I just waited at the edge of the clearing. Finally I called out, "What about your date?"

"The hell with it," he said.

He emerged from the tent wearing old Levis and a tan suede jacket and carrying the decanter and another bottle. He strode over to me and said simply, "All set. Lead the way."

"You certain about this?"

"Where we going?"

"There's a high ridge that looks over the whole valley, but it's a long walk and then a difficult climb."

"Lead on, Deerslayer."

He walked behind me, running into me whenever I slowed down, which was fairly often as there was no trail leading through the woods toward the hills. I knew the general direction, so I led us on what seemed the logical course, veering only to skirt black puddles of melted snow in the underbrush, my flashlight illumining the way ahead.

Griffin stayed right on my heels. After a half hour or so we found ourselves on the mud road. From there I knew every step of the way.

When we finally climbed onto the top crest of the hill, the wind was steady and chill. In the distance we could barely make out the misted pinpoints of the town's lights.

"You've been up here before," Griffin said.

"A few times. It feels sort of haunted. I like it."

"Me too."

Most of the snow had drained off the hilltop, leaving the ground damp and cold. We built a fire, placing twigs directly onto the charred traces of one of my old fires. We didn't stop until we'd collected a reserve supply of sticks and branches and piled them beside the fire. Then we sat down and watched the flames twist and leap in the wind.

For a minute or two Griffin exercised his neck, twisting his head from side to side in rhythm with the orange motions of the flames. Finally he relaxed a little and offered me the brandy. We each took a few swigs.

"This idea you have about leaving," he said. "Is it just to get the hell out of here? Or is it that you want to be someplace else?"

"Both, I don't know. I don't fit here. I want to travel. You've been all over. I've never even been out of the Midwest. I've only seen Ohio, Pennsylvania, and West Virginia—and not much of them."

Seeing him nod, I went on, "For example, I'd like to see the desert, any desert, especially in the spring. I'd like to walk around in every city in America, or at least some of them, Chicago for example. I'd like to swim in the great rivers, or at least see them. There are hundreds of things I'd like to do. I'm fed up with sitting in classes or in my room, reading about what other people have done. I want to do something myself, and not have to follow the same boring schedule every day."

"Routine," Griffin interjected. "You hate routine."

"I'd like to wake up one morning in Tulsa or Dallas, have barbeque for breakfast in some highway place with cowhands, then get on some train and head for California or Oregon or maybe Detroit."

"Detroit is an atrocity."

"I don't care, I'd like to see it—"

"You've been reading too much Whitman," he interrupted. "For Christ's sake I didn't come all the way up here to be serenaded with 'America the Beautiful'."

"That's not what I'm talking about."

"Never mind," he said. "Say you take off tomorrow. Where would you go?"

"No particular place. Wherever the bus goes."

"You'll just get on a bus. Do you know anything at all about traveling? You have any money?"

"A little. I can always find a job."

"Sure you can," he said, dismally. "It's not that simple. I've hitchhiked a lot. It can be surprisingly brutal. You'd better be prepared. You get hungry, very hungry. The police shove you around for being a vagrant. You're always cold and dirty and at the mercy of every psychotic in the world. I'm dead serious. Spend one night in a Greyhound station and you'll know what I'm talking about. If you've been reading that romantic bullshit about traveling, forget it. It's as mythical as *Leaves of Grass*."

"I wasn't planning on hitchhiking right off the bat," I said uncertainly.

"You're a total innocent."

"And you're dead set against traveling," I objected, "but you've already done it. Those adventures did a lot for you. The way I see it, compared to you, well, you already have your own mind and convictions, while I'm still trying to figure things out. For example, say I get off the bus in New York. I've never been there and . . ."

"New York City?" he interrupted.

I nodded enthusiastically.

"Why?" he demanded.

"Why not?"

"Stay the hell away from New York," he said flatly. "It's a death trap, Paul. It would be the end of you."

I didn't get it. I stared at him, waiting for an explanation. In the flickering orange reflections his face looked particularly stern, his eyes squinting.

"I spent last summer in New York," he muttered, "in Greenwich Village, where you'd undoubtedly find yourself. It's obnoxious. Thousands of jerks sitting around in coffee houses and snotty little theaters, bitching about life. All they care about is their own arty whimperings. The whole area is overrun with bullshit philosophers spouting one *ism* or another. Most of them spend their time just sucking in pot smoke and—"

"Pot smoke?"

"Marijuana—some weed that's supposed to give you visions and erotic hallucinations. New York is teeming with potheads, plus all these leftists pissing and moaning about capitalism and how materialistic everything is, how horrible America is, and so on. None of them ever do anything. You'd be a sitting duck."

"I'm that pathetic?"

"You're that naive," he explained, "you know you are." His expression over the flames seemed challenging, obnoxiously challenging.

"You're not in love with New York," I said.

"You're going through something very deep and personal. You're vulnerable, Paul. Plus, you're in some kind of rebellious phase—which is good," he hurriedly added. "Rebellion is great, don't get me wrong, but in New York it would most likely turn sickly and rancid."

He must have noticed my perplexity because he suddenly grinned reassuringly. "Don't look so surprised," he said. "I know what I'm talking about. I went through it myself a few years ago. I can see your future with a certain detachment."

"Is that so?" I said with increasing annoyance.

"Your father is a strong figure," he mused aloud, "whose influence you can't quite—"

"Oh, for God's sake! Knock it off!"

"Let's have some of this," he said, unscrewing the cap from a brown bottle. He held it over the fire long enough to read the label before handing it to me.

"Curaçao," he said as I snatched it. "Ever had it? Lovely beverage."

"Never heard of it."

He took a sip and then another while placing a few more twigs on the fire.

"Tell me," he said in a serious tone. "How balanced are you? The inner you."

I hesitated, my annoyance subsiding as minutes passed in silence.

"I didn't tell you what happened right after the funeral," I said. "Do you want to hear about it, or would you rather go on being this know-it-all jerk?"

"I'm listening," he said.

"After her funeral I was entirely raw, raw to the bone, hurting in every way possible. I went straight down to the river. There's a big steel fretwork bridge over the Ohio River there. About twenty miles to the east two rivers come together in Pittsburgh to form the Ohio River. One is the Monongahela. I forget the other one. Anyway, I climbed up onto the fretwork of this bridge. It was almost dark. The bridge lights were on. Most of the cars and trucks below me had their headlights on. I worked my way up pretty high, nearly to the top. From there I could see a rainstorm approaching, coming up the valley from Pittsburgh toward me. Lights in all the little towns along the river were dimming, then going dark as the storm got closer. The wind was getting stronger, with gusts of rain beating down hard. My hands were cold and wet. The girders were slippery. As rain began lashing onto my face I couldn't tell whether I was crying or it was the rain. Clinging tight to a girder, I was squinting down the valley when all at once I could feel the storm's wild core passing over me, passing through me. The ferocity of it took my breath away. The rain mingled with all the water in my own cells was somehow carrying me far out into the world. I actually felt my own cells scattering with the wind, dispersing themselves all through the world. It was a powerful experience. I don't remember how I got back down."

Griffin had turned away from me. He was looking off to the hills. After a while a train whistle sounded from the distance and slowly waned until it was inaudible.

"How often do you come up here?" he asked.

"I don't know. Now and then."

"I'm sorry, man," he said, in a quiet, confiding tone I hadn't heard from him. "I know you loved her. I guess I got pushed out of shape when you told me so unexpectedly about your leaving. Forget all that junk I said about you and New York. Your girlfriend, was she a classmate?"

"No. Anna was already two years into nursing school. I was working at the steel mill, putting money aside for college. She was so lovely, so gentle and caring and tender. I'd never met anyone like that. She was from Austria. Her father also worked in the mill where I did. They came to the U.S. when she was only four years old. She was curious about everything."

I fell silent and busied myself heaping the rest of the sticks onto the dwindling fire. When it was blazing again, we drew closer to it, sitting beside one another, passing the bottle of orange liqueur back and forth. It had a disgustingly sweet taste but burned nicely going down. After a while Griffin began talking. He didn't go back to anything we'd discussed earlier. He told me about his own childhood, most of which had been in Puerto Rico. His

34

father was a lawyer whose political connections had gotten him a job working for the U.S. State Department in Puerto Rico.

There he'd met Griffin's mother, a native Puerto Rican working as a secretary in San Juan. Their first child was Griffin. A second son died of some tropical ailment at the age of six.

"I think of him every now and then," Griffin said. "I see him in dreams now and then. I wonder what he'd be doing now if he was still alive."

Everything he said interested me. He explained that he'd gone mostly to English-speaking schools for children of U.S. military personnel, yet had played primarily with Puerto Rican kids his age until he was nine, when his family relocated to Ohio. He thought his father was a big shot in the Republican Party. His mother gave bridge parties for politicians and their wives. He told me about impulsive journeys he'd taken through France and Spain, grape-picking jobs in Italy, and brief love affairs all the way from Amsterdam to New Orleans. During his infrequent pauses, I described aspects of my life in Pittsburgh, working the night shift in the steel mill, following the Steelers and the Pirates, eventually planning a family and a future with Anna.

By the time we'd finished off the Curaçao, a stripe of pale pink was expanding along the eastern horizon. Our fire had shrunk to a pile of smoking coals that now and then sputtered under a sudden light drizzle. Our clothes were damp and our legs cramped from the hours of sitting. We were soggy and groggy and slightly drunk, but we had learned a lot about each other's lives. Getting awkwardly to our feet, we stretched sore muscles, grimaced at each other, and finally started hiking back. In prolonged silence we negotiated the perilous stretch of shale, making our way down through dripping birch thickets to the road. There we halted. Griffin yawned and rubbed the back of his neck while I scraped the mud on my shoes off on a rock.

"Throat's raw from so much talk," he said.

"I know."

"I guess you're on your way to catch a bus."

"I might hitch."

"You could always get a tent, share my campsite."

"I'd like that," I said. "But at this point I have to keep moving."

"You have friends in Pittsburgh?"

"Not really."

He nodded, stifling another yawn, and said, "If you get depressed again, write to me, let me know how it's going. Send it to the school here in care of general delivery. I'll be around long enough to finish two more papers. Maybe a month, maybe two."

"Would you write back?"

"Maybe."

"And when you're done here, where will you go?"

He shrugged. "*Adios, amigo. Hasta el próximo.*"

3

Mid-January, 1958, New York City

Nearly one year later—a year spent wandering to various places and working various jobs—I found myself in a furnished room on East 18th Street in Manhattan, near a corner bar called Pete's Tavern. My first nights in the city were spent trying to sleep on the top landing of a building with a broken front door lock. After that came a few nights in the Bowery, stretched out on newspapers on the cement floor of a Salvation Army shelter. The furnished room felt like luxury, despite the dyspeptic radiator and a carpet saturated with mold.

Pete's Tavern was said to be the former home of O. Henry, an American short story writer, an association that appealed to me. I kept meaning to look him up, but the more pressing concern was finding a job. Newspapers stacked in overheated coffee houses had entire sections of help wanted ads. *The New York Herald Tribune* was looking for two press attendants and a copyboy. With a scant week's rent left in my wallet, I put on my single white shirt and hurried over on the subway. It turned out that press attendants had to have experience, so I interviewed for the copyboy position, a late night job, and got it on a trial basis. It paid poorly but the work was easy. During an eight-hour shift, 10 p.m until 6 a.m., I collected the output from two noisy printers—news stories from around the world—and sorted it by topic into editorial baskets scattered around a horseshoe-shaped table. Usually there were two or three editors working late, plus a secretary and sometimes a janitor, but I rarely needed to pester anyone with questions.

By far the most appealing aspect of the job occurred on the way home, when the subway train pulled into Union Square Station. Immediately I'd buy a hot dog—steaming and slathered with ketchup, mustard and chopped onions—and soon I'd feel the fragrant garlicky heat of it in my hands and on my face as I chewed away, trudging through gritty dawn light the few freezing blocks to my room.

As the weeks turned into months, I never lost the sense of being thrilled by New York's astonishing energy and human spectacle, and the endless cultural attractions, the array of museums and libraries, many of them without an entry fee, and the bookstores, the movie theaters—I spent most afternoons and evenings before work wandering around, familiarizing myself with one neighborhood after another. For meals I'd buy a roast beef sandwich in a delicatessen and savor it with a bottle of Seven-Up while strolling and looking.

One afternoon when the weather was too lousy for being outside, the pavement covered with fast hardening slush, sleet falling heavily, I ducked into the nearest movie theater. It was featuring a black and white Scandinavian film about religion and death, but the heater in my room wasn't working, and the theater was pleasantly warm. Movie theaters customarily showed newsreels before the features. This particular newsreel galvanized my attention. It opened with footage of a dozen or so young men with rifles pushing their way through a field of sugar cane. "The rebels in Cuba," boomed an authoritative voiceover, "come down from the mountains and make raids. They burn the cane fields. These men are called *los barbudos*, the bearded ones. Led by young lawyer Fidel Castro, they are causing a serious problem for President Fulgencio Batista, a good friend of the United States." The music swelled. The screen filled with a photo of Fidel Castro, beardless, wearing a white shirt and sport coat, standing on a city sidewalk. Most of the *barbudos* in the footage were actually clean-shaven. This struck me, as did the startling look of earnest purpose on their young faces. While there were three or four older men among them, in their late twenties or early thirties, with long hair and beards, most of the rebels looked to be in their teens or barely into their twenties. They were thin and athletic, fervent, their skins the tones of mingled races, bringing to mind many of the younger guys I'd worked with in the steel mill, the only place in my experience, except for team sports, where brown and black and white guys associated without a lot of stress. The final image on the newreels was a middle-aged fat man in sunglasses and a flowery necktie, sitting at a big desk. He had obtrusive jowls and was scowling: *Presidente* Batista.

This was exciting. It was unsettling. Mind racing, I sat through the entirety of that Scandinavian movie again, basically oblivious to it, distracted throughout by the images I'd just seen of the Caribbean island. As other movie-goers filed out I stayed in my seat to catch that newsreel once again. What stayed with me most deeply when I finally left the theater was something conveyed by Fidel Castro's face—an impression of exceptional intelligence and purity of resolve—a lot to presume from a few seconds' screen presence. That and the seeming harmony of different races sharing a common purpose, being fully alive, something Albert Camus had written about. There was a civil rights movement going on, mostly in southern states. My own meager experience with it had been in Pittsburgh, where there was a widely shared conviction that discrimination was not wanted. I had been to black churches with high school friends. We frequently ate at one another's homes and played basketball, football and baseball together. We worked side by side in the same jobs. I'd never heard anyone except my parents criticize interracial dating. I couldn't recall ever being taught anything about Latin American or Caribbean history, apart from a few incidents in which North Americans were invariably portrayed as the virtuous side, such as the Alamo. I had only a dim notion of where Cuba was, yet I found myself increasingly intrigued, almost obsessed. Those young Cubans were fighting for their future, and I urgently wanted to know more. The fact they were risking their lives to change their country was powerfully if inexplicably compelling.

The next few shifts at the *Herald Tribune* I spent my breaks in what they called the morgue: a large room in which old editions of the paper were stored, along with reference books, maps, and various dispatches archived by editors. There wasn't much about contemporary Cuba, apart from occasional stories about celebrities enjoying Havana's nightlife, but there were maps of the island. I was startled to discover it was less than one hundred miles from Florida. In the following days I checked several bookstores but found only travel guides praising particular beaches and profiling Ernest Hemingway. Not a word about the current rebellion.

At one point one of the senior editors, seeing me searching through the morgue, asked what I was looking for. I told him I was hoping to find some coverage of the rebellion in Cuba. He told me that while the *Herald Tribune* coverage was "perhaps unimpressive," our rival, *The New York Times,* had scored a major journalistic scoop earlier by running an article by reporter Herbert Matthews that was essentially an interview with Fidel Castro done in the Sierra Maestra mountains in eastern Cuba. He went on to say that Batista had denounced the story, calling it a hoax and claiming Castro was dead. I felt immensely lucky to find out about this interview and about yet another story by Matthews complete with photos of him in the mountains with Fidel.

The editor told me that Matthews had openly declared his support for the rebel leader as well as his sense that Fidel's crusade would prove victorious. This so intrigued me that the editor promised he'd phone an acquaintance at the *Times* and ask for a print-out of both stories for me. I don't know whether he followed up or not, but I never got them, and from then on he seemed to be avoiding me.

When I was initially hired by the paper, I'd sent a postcard to Griffin care of the college. I should have gotten his parents' address. Two weeks later I sent another postcard to general delivery at the college, urging him to get in touch. This time I heavily underlined my address. A vague idea was already coming into focus and I wanted Griffin to be part of it.

Over the next few days I got a library card and spent time in the main public library, where they had number of books and news articles about Cuba. Taking breaks from that, I spent hours in the Metropolitan Museum of Art. I loved the lower Second Avenue delicatessens with the glass cases on their counters filled with beautiful roast beefs and chocolate layer cakes. It seemed healthiest to be either entirely outdoors or entirely indoors, as interiors of buses and subways were preposterously overheated for people in hefty winter clothes.

After one bitterly cold, bright day wandering in Central Park, I walked back downtown and encountered a pale young woman in blue jeans and a brown leather jacket sitting on the steps to my apartment building, her jaw cupped in gloved hands. She was partially blocking the stairs. After pausing a moment, I started up, edging awkwardly around her. She seemed thoroughly pre-occupied.

"Next door," she said, "in the bar, using the restroom, your friend."

She had dark brown hair, full lips and surprisingly dark blue eyes. While she wasn't exactly beautiful, there was certainly something striking about her, something exotic.

"Sorry," I said, "did you just say 'my friend?'"

"You *are* Paul Bell, aren't you? You have to be. He said you looked like the most earnest person on earth."

"Griffin?" I exclaimed, "You know Griffin?"

"Ricky," she said with a quick bright smile as she stood up, extending a hand. "I call him Ricky."

I caught her hand. "Paul," I said.

"Rachel Greenberg," she said, taking my hand.

Then I saw Griffin hurrying along the sidewalk toward us, looking very different, somewhat better-looking with his hair grown out all curly and black, bareheaded in the cold.

"Paul, I'll be damned." He seized my hand for a second and then threw his arms around me in a fierce bearhug. I laughed and pounded him on the back.

"Jesus," he said. "No kidding." He held me at arm's length and looked me over from oxblood shoes to brown corduroy jacket to my recent haircut. "You're looking amazingly prosperous, man! Good to see you!"

"I tried to reach you—"

"Come on." He yanked me along the sidewalk while Rachel hurried to keep up. "You're coming to our apartment," he said. "You've met Precious Cargo here. We'll have a meal, a real meal. Wait," he said, halting us. "Let's get a cup of coffee. We have to talk."

"We'll see you there, okay?" he said to Rachel. "Back at your place."

She looked momentarily hurt or confused, but then shrugged and walked away.

Griffin turned us around and started us back along Second Avenue, talking all the way to a small delicatessen where we swung onto two stools and he ordered us coffees.

"Damn," he said. "Just how the hell are you? What have you been doing?"

"Mostly scrambling from job to job," I said. "I guess you got my card. I wasn't sure how to find you."

"Got a quarter?" he interrupted.

A clerk carefully set two brimming cups of coffee down in front of us. I fumbled some change out of my pocket and handed it to Griffin. He punched me lightly on the shoulder, spun off his stool and strode over to the cashier by the door. A moment later he returned, puffing jauntily on a cigarillo.

"Listen," I said urgently. "I've got to tell you this plan. I've been thinking about it day and night and it has me seriously excited. You've got to see this newsreel I saw. I've been thinking about going there, and it would be great if you'd go with me, but before I get way into it, you'd better tell me what you're doing. Are you serious about this girl? Rachel? I thought you detested New York."

"I do, trust me, but this is definitely where the action is, and Rachel's helping me out. I'm crashing at her place."

"Do you have a job?"

He slipped the pack of cigarillos into his shirt pocket. "A job," he chuckled derisively, "You have no idea how tough it is here. I'm in line for an audition at Actors' Studio, and I'm studying dance with José Limon. But it's a bitch to do anything without connections in this rat bastard of a city. You still trying to write? Mrs Guss missed you, you know."

"I sent her postcards," I protested, "at least every month or so."

"You did? Listen, I wanted you to meet Rachel but I need to clue you in on a couple of things first. It's like this. I live like a thorough bastard here. If you're going to survive in New York you have to be one son-of-a-bitch."

"How so?" I said.

"It's hard to explain but my scruples are shot to hell. You're something of a straight arrow, so I doubt you'd understand, but the thing with Rachel is problematic, you'll see."

"Explain."

"I've been trying to help her," he began again, "to straighten her out. It sounds corny, but she needs me. About a year ago she got all disoriented by some quack analyst. I've been doing my best to plug her back into the real world again."

A group of Italian women dressed in fur coats were just coming in, arguing loudly. He scowled at them as I paid the bill. We stepped out into the cold, joining the moving crowd on the sidewalk. Finally Griffin stopped in front of an old brick building near Sheridan Square. The fire escapes were being painted orange. Three workers were cleaning brushes on the front steps, preparing to quit for the day.

"Just one thing I need to mention," Griffin said, edging us past the painters and into a dim hallway. "Rachel thinks an old love of mine was killed in a hit and run accident last year while I was at school. She might ask you about it. All you have to know is that I fell apart and you helped put me back together again. All right? She likes you already, because you gave me a hand then."

While he was talking I came to a full stop in the hall, bewildered.

"Come on," he said flatly, "let's go up."

"Wait a minute," I said. "Just in case Rachel asks, what might be the name of this love of yours?"

"I told her it was Anna, and she came from Austria. A failure of imagination, I suppose."

"Anna," I repeated, stunned by his admission. "A failure of something, that's for sure. Why in hell would you do that? "

"Don't take it personally, Paul. I know it's weird, but you don't understand this town."

He turned and started up the stairs. I followed, wondering what his motive could possibly be for telling such a lie. At the fifth floor he knocked on the first door. We waited in silence until Rachel opened it to us.

"We're starving," Griffin said in a jaunty tone. She nodded, and we watched her walk into the tiny kitchen, hips rolling nicely in tight Levis. I guessed her to be about nineteen. As a result perhaps of being so generously built, she moved a little clumsily, a little self-consciously, and she wasn't very articulate, but such faint defects disappeared in the enormous attraction her Jewish sensuality had for a Midwesterner like myself. Her eyes alone were different than any I'd ever seen. Large and unusually deep blue and set wide apart, they seemed peculiarly reflective of her feelings.

Griffin grinned at me. "Make something special, Rachel," he called after her.

She regarded us from the kitchen, "I'm making spaghetti."

"Could you run out and get some decent wine, something better than that rot-gut Chianti?" Griffin asked. She looked dismayed.

"Anything's fine," I said. "I shouldn't have alcohol anyway. I have to be at work by ten."

"Pity," Griffin said. His voice dropped conspiratorially as we stopped in the small living room. The walls were hung with fading Chagall prints.

"I've been here about five months now," he went on. "We met in a little coffee house on Bleeker. I was sitting there and Rachel was at the table next to mine, supposedly reading. At first she just gave me this worried frown, but almost immediately we were on our way here. I've been here ever since. You take the couch."

He fiddled with the knobs on an expensive-looking record player. A jazz trumpet sounded from two speakers set in a small bookcase.

"Stereo," he said. "Just listen to that." He flopped into a chair, stretched out his legs and expansively lit another cigarillo. Puffing languidly, he gave me a long, appraising look.

"Sit down, Paul," he said. "How long've you been in town?"

"About two months."

"So what have you been up to?"

"I'm working as a copyboy for the *New York Herald Tribune.*"

"No! Say it isn't so! A lackey for the major media! Shame, Paul, *shame!* But don't talk to me about jobs. Everyone I know bitches incessantly about their job. Not one of them has the guts to quit."

"Listen to me for a second," I interrupted. "I have an idea that might actually interest you. In fact, you're a major part of what I have in mind." Describing the newsreel involving Cuba, I tried to convey how fiercely I'd felt the energy that bound together those young rebels. I stressed the hunger I felt for that. Somewhat surprised to find him genuinely paying attention, I went on to relate details of my job at the paper, how it included access to maps and even press cards. While he listened without interrupting, he showed no response apart from an occasional nod indicating he was taking it all in.

"So," I concluded, "I guess it's obvious where I'm going with this—I'm hoping you'll come with me. We would be reporters. You up for a fantastic adventure?"

"Fantastic," he agreed sardonically. "The very word."

"Come on, man. Think about it. We could do this. I could probably get us press passes. We'd be doing something real with our lives. I know you understand what I mean."

He was silent, noncommittal.

46

"Well? What are you thinking?" I asked anxiously, leaning toward him.

"I'm remembering how Puerto Ricans felt about *yanquis* when I was a kid. In fact, I still get treated in shabby racist ways here in this town. We islanders aren't genuine Americans, you know, not really. I promise you, those revolutionaries in Cuba don't want you or any other *yanquis* coming around. Why would they? Cubans know Americans as tourists, *ricos*, people lording it over them. It's just like Puerto Rico there, it would have to be."

He paused and leaned back against a pillow for a moment before lunging forward again. "It's standard practice for this country, your country, to maintain some dictator to oversee things, to hold things in check for Wall Street. Look what happened in Guatemala. Any of the dispatches at your newspaper ever mention that?"

"You know," I said, "For a guy so proud of living in isolation, you sure think you know everything about everything."

"Well, maybe I do know some things."

"And maybe you don't know some things," I interrupted. "Anyway, we'd be going as journalists. You could be a photographer. I might be able to get a camera for you from the newspaper."

"I have a camera," he snapped. "But tell me this. Do you know even one single person who has ever been to Cuba?"

He was far more negative than I had anticipated. This was surprising and very disappointing. I thought the sheer adventure of it all would appeal to him.

"You want me aboard because I speak Spanish, right? Obviously you need a translator. As far as I know, your prowess in Spanish hovers around zero."

"True, but that's not the only reason I want to do this with you. You're my friend, Griffin. At this point, you're my only friend. Please consider it. We'd be doing something

47

real in the world, something serious, besides having a tremendous adventure."

He wasn't responding at all, just staring at the floor, when Rachel appeared in the doorway.

"Excuse me, Ricky, dinner's almost ready."

"Bravo," he said, springing up. "Come on, Paul."

I followed him into the kitchen, a depressingly small room, yet it had a window. Dusk was already silhouetting the brick buildings outside. Rachel had resumed stirring a pan of bubbling noodles in a darkness lessened only by the flames of the gas stove.

"He tells me you're an actress," I said.

Griffin had gone back to get another chair.

"I was in two plays, both off-Broadway. Just minor roles. I wasn't very good."

"You were beautiful," Griffin contradicted her, sliding a third chair under a card table by the window. She switched on a dim overhead light. He found the Chianti bottle under the sink, extracted a tasseled cork and sloshed wine into three chipped coffee cups.

"Hideous stuff," he said.

Her expression was impassive as she leaned over us and dished out the spaghetti. I was pleased by her quiet way of filling our plates without any questions, as though I were an old friend whose appetite she knew. As she sat down then, tossing that heavy skein of hair back over her slender shoulders, Griffin raised his cup.

"Here's to two great people," he said. "Hey, Rachel, any chance you have a friend who might be just right for Paul?"

He drained his cup before Rachel or I managed a sip.

"Let me think about it," she replied.

"Please don't," I said, shaking my head. "I'm not ready yet."

The spaghetti was slightly undercooked but the sauce had a rich, ripe tomato flavor. I was vigorously on my third mouthful when Griffin poured himself a second cup of

Chianti, took a long swallow, and suddenly glared at Rachel.

"The spaghetti is raw," he snapped. "Did you cook it in the refrigerator?"

Rachel looked stricken.

"Take some of mine," I said. "It's fully cooked. It's perfect."

"Let's go find a couple of steaks, Paul. This is indigestible."

"I'm not leaving a full plate of good food," I insisted.

"Come on," he said, getting to his feet. "Let's get out of here."

"I'm sorry," Rachel said in a miserable tone. "I can cook it some more, Ricky. I thought you liked it *al dente*. Let me have your plate."

"Paul, let's go." He disappeared into the bedroom.

I just sat still, bewildered, watching Rachel glumly dump the contents of his plate into the garbage pail. When she reached for mine, I held onto it and began eating again. I was trying to think of something to say when Griffin reappeared, wearing a leather jacket, looking bewilderingly cheerful.

"You coming?" he said.

"Nah. I'll just finish this and find the subway," I said. "I have to be at work in an hour, and I'm really enjoying the spaghetti. Despite your fantastic rudeness."

He shook his head disbelievingly and said, "Suit yourself. Just be sure to leave us your address."

"You know where I live. Next to O'Henry's Tavern. But before you go lurching off—how about we plan on the three of us taking the boat cruise around the island, once it warms up, my treat. Sound good?"

"Incredible," he said, shaking his head. "You haven't changed a bit."

I turned to Rachel. "What do you think? We could take a thermos of hot coffee."

She looked to Griffin for her answer.

"We're not going on any insipid tourist cruise," he said flatly.

"Maybe just you and me then, Rachel," I suggested. "Griffin can spend the time getting his brain examined."

She chuckled mirthlessly. He ran a hand down through her hair, tugging her head back gently and lightly kissing her throat.

"I've never been on that cruise," she said. "It sounds like fun. Paul, I think I have a friend you might like. Her name is Cynthia and—"

"I don't think so," I interrupted her. "But thanks for the offer. I do appreciate it."

"Okay, children," Griffin said. "I'll be back soon. Watch out for this guy, Rachel." He cuffed me on the shoulder and was gone. I heard his footsteps on the stairs. A moment later the record-player clicked, paused, and the jazz trumpet sounded again.

Otherside we continued eating in awkward silence. The sound of a siren rose abruptly and faded away until I could hear Rachel's quiet breathing.

"So," I ventured at last, "you're from New York?"

"Bronx." Then more silence.

"Does he often erupt like that?" I asked.

"He's temperamental. What were you two talking about?"

"Nothing much," I said. "Future possibilities."

"You were good to him at school," she said. "He told me about you, how you consoled him when Anna died."

I scraped my chair a little sideways in order to see her face.

"I know I'm not on his level," she began again, in the same preoccupied tone, "but you know how he is. He's got a lot going on."

"Really? Such as?"

"He likes you a lot," she said. "He told me so."

"He's complicated."

"He's a very good person," she said quickly, "but he's frustrated. He can't stand the thought of wasting his life, yet he can't think of anything that wouldn't be wasting it. My mother thinks he has a superiority complex."

I chuckled.

"I want to help him keep his spirits up," she said. "He says I'm the only person that's ever truly understood him. Like you said, he's complicated."

We began clearing the table. She washed the dishes under the tap and I dried them. She talked a bit about her life prior to Griffin and she asked about mine. I didn't say much. I couldn't tell her about Anna, thanks to Griffin, and there wasn't much else worth discussing. Griffin still hadn't returned by the time I had to leave. She tried again to apologize for the spaghetti but stopped when I impulsively and clumsily hugged her.

* * *

A week passed before I saw Griffin again. Three storeys below my window hard kernels of sleet were pelting down, darkening the late afternoon, annoying but not quite halting the crew of Con Edison workmen in the street. They went right on tearing up wet macadam. In spite of the racket of pneumatic drills, I was trying to memorize the unpronounceable place names on a map of Cuba spread over the table when I heard someone beating on a door farther down the corridor. I opened to see Griffin, sleet in his hair, an Air France bag slung over one of his shoulders.

He handed me the bag and unzipped his jacket. "I'm on my way to dance class. Not interrupting any creative endeavors, am I?" He dropped the jacket on the floor and started poking through the newspaper clippings strewn over my map of Cuba.

"Have a seat," I said. "How's Rachel? You finally manage to apologize?"

"She's very forgiving. By the way, she seems to have adopted you. She sent you some goodies there in my bag."

He picked up several clippings from the table and dropped into the armchair by the window and began reading. I opened the bag and found on top of his leotards a sticky packet of cherry pastries wrapped in aluminum foil.

"It's too dark in here to read," he said.

"It's about to snow," I agreed, turning on the table lamp, the only light in the entire apartment.

"These cherry things for me?"

"Don't pretend to be surprised." He flipped the clippings back onto the map.

"Hand me that carton of milk," I said, "behind you, outside on the sill."

He said something as he twisted around to open the window get the carton, but his words were drowned out in the roar of drills.

"I've been wanting to talk to you," I said. "Have you thought more about my idea for us?"

He leaned forward in the chair and said, "And I've been wanting to talk to you—these newspapers and the other stuff you've been reading. I'm sure they say the usual crap, what a bastard Batista is, how oppressive, how the Cubans want to get rid of yet another dictator. Let me tell you what's really going on. They're having a bloody rebellion down there simply because Uncle Sam has been sucking Cuba dry for a hundred years. That's what's this is all about. Get it? You're an American. You're the enemy."

"Maybe it's not that simple," I said patiently. "We could get some good interviews. "Maybe they're trying to overturn their government because it's corrupt, it's vicious. I don't believe it's all about the USA. I'll bet it's much more like the Spanish Civil War, a truly great cause. The Nazis supported Franco. So did the Italian fascists. That's where the Second World War started. I've been reading about this."

He looked as though he might concede this possibility.

"Anyway, we should go and see for ourselves," I said. "We could report on it. The rebels might want us to write about them. They've welcomed other journalists."

"Like I said," he replied, "you're the original innocent abroad, although you've never been abroad. What makes you think we could get anywhere near the action?"

Sleet peppered the window behind him. Seeing I wasn't answering, he reached over and picked up one of the clippings he'd glanced at earlier. It was a black and white magazine photo of Fidel Castro looking solemn behind a dark beard. He was standing in a field of young sugar cane, holding a rifle with a telescopic sight. Griffin examined the photo intently for several minutes.

"Here's a guy fighting his own private war against the way things are, the way things always have been, the way things always will be. And you want to get close to that?"

"Do you know who Richard Harding Davis is?"

"Why do I suspect you're yearning to tell me?"

"He's a journalist," I said. "He threw himself into things. He took risks. He wrote. That's what I want to do. We could interview Castro. You could take photos. You don't like things as they are any more than I do. There's no place for us here. You know that. We're both trying to adapt to a society we don't much like. Let's get out of it. Wouldn't you like to report on a revolution?"

Shaking his head, he set the clipping back with the others and said, "You want to go to Cuba. Rachel wants to work on a kibbutz. I just want to dance."

"At school you seemed like an honest-to-god rebel," I said. "Is that phase all over? You all grown up now?"

He stood up, reached for his wet jacket, slipped one arm into it, and slapped me on the knee. I tilted the milk carton to my mouth and drank, saying nothing.

"It's not as if either of us has any money," he said. "Or any contact of any kind with any revolutionary movement."

I tossed the carton at the waste basket. He planted one foot on the sill and leaned on his knee, staring out through the sleet at the street below. The building trembled slightly with the underground rumble of the subway far beneath it. Everything was briefly quiet. The Con Edison guys must have stopped for the day.

"Have you told anyone else about this?" he asked.

"Just you."

I watched the back of his head and wondered what was going on inside it. He remained absolutely still, gazing out at the sleet and the slick reflections of red and yellow neon shimmering along the wet pavement. I knew exactly what he could see from that window.

Finally, his back still to me, he said, "I've got to get going." He straightened, zipped up his jacket, and slipped his bag over his shoulder. "It seems you really need me," he said. "You realize you could never do this without me."

"So it seems."

Leaving the door open, without another word he started down the corridor.

4

Late February, 1958

I dropped my rucksack on the floor next to the information booth in the Port Authority Bus Terminal and looked around for Griffin. I'd given notice at the *Herald Tribune*. In the time I still had left to work I'd managed to get hold of two blank press passes and fit them with pictures we'd taken at a dime store photo booth. They looked reasonably official. In the bus terminal there were dozens of soldiers and sailors in uniform, plus hundreds of commuters rushing along clutching briefcases. Everyone seemed to be in a hurry. With a departure schedule in hand, I carried my rucksack over to a snack bar, took a seat at the counter and ordered a glass of milk and a Danish. Swiveling on the seat, I continued surveying the crowd until a waitress set a cup of black coffee and a plate of burnt toast down in front of me.

"That's not my order," I said to her. Without a word or even a glance, she ripped a check off her pad and slid it under my saucer, then hurried away. I nibbled at the dry toast and with increasing apprehension kept an eye on the big clock over the information booth. Every few minutes a loudspeaker announced another bus departing. A full hour must have passed before I finally saw Griffin, snow melting in his hair and shoulders, pushing his way through the crowd.

"*Buenos días, hombre!*" he said excitedly. "You check the buses yet?"

"You're late. Is everything all right?"

"Couldn't be better. How soon can we get out of here?"

"Right away," I said. "They have about twenty buses heading south every hour."

"In that case we have time for breakfast." He slid onto the stool next to mine and glanced at the remains of my toast. "Glad to see you're dieting. That's a habit that should come in handy. What's the matter? Think I wouldn't show up?"

He ordered a large orange juice, scrambled eggs, an English muffin with butter and marmalade, and coffee.

"Foreign intrigue gives a man an appetite," he said happily. "Sorry to be late. Rachel held me up."

"You eat amazingly well for a pauper. How is Rachel?"

"Even the penniless must eat. Rachel's fine. She'll survive. She gave us some money. Not much. Her folks will probably send her to Israel. This your pack?"

"Yeah, but listen," I said. "I've got fifty-five dollars. That should get us somewhere."

"You'll have to lighten that load. It looks heavy."

"Books mostly, Dos Passos, Kenneth Patchen. I can carry it. It's not that bad."

The waitress brought his breakfast exactly as he'd ordered it, accompanied by four pats of butter and two little paper cups of marmalade. I went to ask about fares. and was soon back, waving two tickets to D.C. He was right—a bus all the way to Florida was too expensive.

"No sweat," he said when I told him. "Let's just get our asses to D.C. From there we'll improvise. There should be thousands of New Yorkers driving to Florida. We can stay for free in YMCAs."

He finished his coffee and added, "I know a girl in Miami who'll be delighted to put us up. It'll be great."

"Let's not do any lingering in Miami."

"Let's just get ourselves there."

"Eight minutes to departure," I said.

We snatched our bags and ran to the gate where a silver, mud-spattered bus was warming up, sending clouds of exhaust into the frosty air. The driver was already collecting tickets from a line of passengers, most of them taking seats in the front.

Going all the way to the back, I shoved my rucksack into the rack over one of the last seats. Griffin flopped down beside me just as the motor growled loudly into action directly beneath our seat. The heavy air-brakes hissed to a release and we began rolling slowly backward, maneuvering into the exit lane. I took a deep breath that smelled of dust and orange peels. Griffin let out a relieved sigh, and the big Trailblazer swung expertly into city traffic.

"*Adiós*, New York," Griffin muttered. "You rat-hole of a city."

"Here we go," I enthused. The bus picked up speed and was soon flanked by the white tiles of the Lincoln Tunnel. As the interior lights came on, Griffin gave me a vigorous smack on the thigh.

"I'll miss Rachel," he said. "She's not entirely pleased about your stealing me away."

"You told her where we're going?"

"I did. She thinks it's crazy, but she's glad I have some solid plan."

I was concentrating on concealing my exultation. Not easy, as I was almost shuddering with excitement. We were actually on our way to Cuba—charging into an unknown future, to a place very unlike Eisenhower's glum America. The bus barrelled straight down the highway through New Jersey's industrial marshland. Soon we were cruising along the turnpike into Philadelphia.

During a ten-minute rest stop we managed to buy a couple of Hershey bars and Pepsis before the bus took off again, devouring mileage, slowing only for toll stations. We sped across the northern tip of Delaware and then on down through Maryland. The scenery had a monotonous sameness. Billboards and telephone poles whipped past at an invariable sixty-five miles an hour.

Griffin dozed off, but I remained awake. Looking out at the hills and barren fields, I thought of all the bus travel I'd done before getting to New York. Many different individuals had enlivened the seat beside me with monologues about their families, their religious beliefs or their concerns about Russia's latest space shot. Never had there been someone in that seat who seemed to me truly amiable. I recalled those stretches of loneliness and boredom in an oddly vivid way, enjoying all the more the silent presence of Griffin sleeping fitfully beside me. When we finally pulled into DC, snow was falling from an ashen sky. It lent a certain lightness to the squat massive structures dominating the Capitol, blurring the hard edges, softening things, animating that ponderous atmosphere of power in much the same way cherry blossoms would in another month or so. We emerged from the depot wanting to stretch our legs yet wincing at the shock of freezing air. It was nearly dark.

"Ever been here?" Griffin asked. We were walking along a wide avenue. Cars were speeding by, many of them limousines. We seemed to be the only pedestrians.

"Never." I replied. "You?"

"A long time ago," he said. "Family trip to the Smithsonian."

"There's a cop on the corner," I interrupted. "We can ask directions. We need to find a place before the missions get packed. With luck we might even get some free supper."

"You sound experienced," he said doubtfully.

Streetlights blinked on just as we arrived at the blue neon cross above the front doors of the Holy Redeemer Mission. The desk clerk was a bald old man with reddened, watery eyes. He explained that they didn't serve food and all the rooms were booked.

"So this isn't really a Christian institution," Griffin said to him.

"Sir?" the clerk said.

"I mean," Griffin went on, "this is a huge building. It must have some space in it. We don't need beds. We can sleep anywhere. We'll be gone first thing in the morning."

"Are you servicemen? Students?"

"Neither," Griffin said testily, "but you must have something available."

The clerk picked up a brochure from the counter and held it out, "Here's what's available." In a flash of temper Griffin snatched the brochure, crumpled it, and bounced it off the clerk's forehead.

We were soon standing outside.

"I saw a White Castle back there," Griffin said. "Let's eat and take it from there."

His flare of anger, already sharply reduced, had vanished entirely by the time we got to the hamburger joint. I noticed in the window a 'Whites Only' sign, but I didn't mention it to Griffin. His mood was too precarious. We each downed two cheeseburgers with fries and a chocolate milkshake. Luckily the waitress overheard our conversation and knew exactly where the nearest Salvation Army Mission was. We thanked her and left a modest tip.

In charge at the mission was a muscular black man with a handsome gray beard. He gave us forms to fill out before leading us down a corridor to a flight of stairs that led to an enormous room bathed in fluorescent light. I caught my breath, stunned by the stench—a mingling of vomit, unwashed bodies, and some sickeningly strong disinfectant.

"God Almighty," Griffin muttered.

We were standing on a concrete floor almost entirely covered by some forty or fifty individuals of various races sprawled on scattered sheets of newspaper. Most were sleeping, while others were talking, some to themselves, or moaning, or weeping. Most appeared to be fully dressed, some with earmuffs, gloves, and shabby overcoats. Under the harsh light their faces and hands were the mottled colors of flesh too long exposed to bad weather, bad alcohol, and God only knows what diseases.

"We suggest you keep your shoes on," the director said to us. "I'm sorry to say we've had incidents of theft." He motioned us toward a stack of newspapers on a bench against the far wall. We remained at the foot of the stairs. There seemed to be no heat source other than that imparted by the mass of bodies. An amputee dressed only in a tee shirt and a pair of filthy shorts was curled up, snoring loudly. Near him was an old African-American guy clutching a filthy blanket.

"Over here, please," the director called to us.

I looked at Griffin.

"Let's get out of here," he said.

I nodded, unable to imagine falling asleep in that environment.

We gave our polite regrets before scrambling back up the stairs, down the hallway and back into the frigid night air. We kept moving, wanting to put as much distance as possible between us and that disease incubation center.

"I stayed at a mission in the Bowery several nights," I told Griffin. "It wasn't anything like that place."

"You think a few of those bodies might have been dead?" Griffin asked.

"Who knows?"

"Right in the heart of the capital of the richest country on earth," he said.

We walked on, striding fast to keep warm. Now and then a taxi slowed, cruising along the curb beside us. We waved them all on. It was almost midnight when we found ourselves passing a particularly imposing structure. We stopped, side by side, and gazed up at the luminous cavern above us—the Lincoln Memorial. The city was entirely hushed. Repositioning our bags, we trudged up the wide stretch of steps to stand beneath the immense seated figure. We set down our bags, slid our hands into our pockets and stood in silence, protected from the winds swirling around outside. A guard approached and paused, looking us over before walking away without a word. We kept staring up at that stark, solemn figure, one of the few presidents for whom we both had deep respect. The dramatic spotlighting revealed every crease on his gaunt face, and on the words chiseled into the wall behind him. One of his hands was clenched in a fist, while the other was at rest, suggesting both strength and compassion.

"All men are born equal," said Griffin.

"Created," I said. "All men are created equal. My high school class had to memorize the Gettysburg Address—*it is for us the living . . .*"

"You must have had a good teacher."

I nodded, remembering.

"Here's to you, Abe," Griffin said quietly. "You gave it your all."

The feeling was personal reverence—in my case partly due to the story of his having slept on the wintry grave of a childhood sweetheart, partly due to what I knew of what came later, his challenge to the South, his insistence on emancipation.

"If I had a hat," Griffin said. "I would take it off."

"Think he'd approve of what we're doing?"

Griffin didn't respond. A chalky plume of breath was the sole indication he wasn't as frozen as the statue.

"Hard to know," he said at last. "He tried to change things. He had to be killed."

* * *

61

The surface of the snow-swollen Potomac was a dull charcoal grey under a heavily overcast sky when we left DC early in the morning, bleary-eyed and edgy from spending the night pretending not to be sleeping in an all-night restaurant mostly for truckers. Standing beside the highway we held out our thumbs and waited. After about half an hour a blue Buick sedan came to a halt some yards ahead of us. We grabbed our bags and ran. Peering back at us from the driver's seat was a very short woman probably in her seventies, perched on two cushions, tightly gripping the wheel. She had curly pale blue hair and a huge swelling in the front of her neck. I'd never seen blue hair. I'd never seen such a swelling on a neck.

"Since you're staring," she said icily, "it's a goiter." She was watching me in the rearview mirror, touching her neck with a fluttering gesture.

"It's the Negro air," she said. "That's what provokes your goiters. Lots of folks have them. That's a scientific fact."

Griffin had an expression of deeply offended incredulity, but he remained quiet.

She seemed to be a competent driver. I leaned back and drowsily watched the passing series of Burma Shave rhymes posted along the highway. I was almost asleep when her voice startled me awake.

"There's no way on God's good earth," she was saying, "that I would ever have picked you up if I didn't have to go through all this darkie country."

Griffin didn't respond.

"Y'all appear to be nice boys," she went on. "You surely don't seem like Yankees."

"Thank you, Ma'am," Griffin said. 'Mighty kind of you. Mighty kind."

When I woke again hours later the Buick's tires were scraping a curb. Griffin immediately began setting our bags out on the sidewalk.

"Welcome to South Carolina, young Master Bell," he said, "I'm amazed you could sleep through her endless insane tirades."

Griffin thought she was a full-blown lunatic. I thought she was just another lonely, run-of-the mill racist.

"Maybe so," he said. "But it's no damn wonder Eisenhower had to send in the National Guard so little kids could go to school."

We watched her drive away, relieved to be rid of her and grateful to be almost halfway to Florida.

* * *

An all-important trick in successfully hitching is to get your lifts well before dark. At night there's no chance. All afternoon we watched cars speed past without any sign of their drivers seeing us. Alternating the job of thumbing so one of us could keep his hands warming his ears, we shuffled our feet for circulation and swore with increasing frustration. Then came a brief period of cars pulling to the curb and looking us over before abruptly driving off. Finally got a number of rides, short ones, until a farmer in a large truck hauled us nearly ninety miles. When he abruptly turned onto a dusty gravel road leading through fields of okra, we asked to be let off. We lugged our bags back to the highway and resumed thumbing, walking along the road's shoulder until yet another ride took us another fifty miles and left us in a small town. We found our way to a diner and a welcome meal of fried fish sandwiches and vegetable soup. Parked just outside the diner was a black, highly polished Chevy Bel Air convertible. As we emerged, a guy wearing sunglasses and a black leather windbreaker was briskly rubbing dead bugs off the windshield. We admired his car, an extravagant vehicle with gleaming chrome exhaust pipes, flashy hubcaps and the word *Stanmobile* painted in gold stars across the trunk.

"Hey, Stan," Griffin ventured, "You've got one diabolic machine there. Where's it going?"

The guy slowly looked us over. "All the way down and down to party town," he said. "Key West, the absolute best."

"We're going to Miami," I spoke up. "Want passengers?"

"Climb on in," Stan said, stuffing his rag under the front seat. "Bags go in the trunk. Let's get to it, gents. Black Beauty is pawing the turf."

He kept the radio going with rock music, changing stations whenever a commercial came on. The blaring music and the top being down—the night air rushing past us—thwarted any attempts at conversation. We took turns driving, keeping that sleek Stanmobile at just the speed limit, more or less 65 mph, refilling the gas tank twice, each paid by Stan without complaint. Several cars and one long distance trucker sounded their horns and waved in appreciation. We laughed, waved back, and sailed smoothly on. The night felt like a beautiful dream: the music, the wind, the glittering stars, the varying aromas, the miles falling away . . .

Early morning found us standing in wet sand somewhere north of Miami Beach, watching the waves foam around our ankles. Stan was managing to get the convertible top up. In the humid dawn light a heavy mist was falling onto a pale green sea. It was just warm enough for Griffin and me to be stripped down to sopping underpants. Swimming in the rain had seemed ridiculous to Non-stop Stan.

"Sure you don't want to stick around?" Griffin asked him.

"Gotta run," he replied. "I take it you guys are broke. Buy you breakfast?"

"You've already done enough for the cause," I said, shaking hands with him. "Take care of yourself and Black Beauty."

"Count on it," Stan replied and drove away.

Griffin and I ambled up the beach to a roped-off section marked 'Hotel Patrons Only.' A number of damp canvas chairs were arranged on the sand, some under striped umbrellas. We retrieved our clothes from under a beach chair, pulled them on, and made our way to a tourist street lined with well-heeled, pastel-toned resort hotels. Everything was still quiet, except for delivery trucks and a few taxis. Griffin went off to use a pay phone to call his friend Marsha. I went over to a row of newspaper stands and used two dimes to get copies of the *New York Times* and the *Miami Herald,* in hopes of finding news about Cuba. Nothing in the *Times.* The *Herald* had several display ads for Havana nightclubs, and one for deep sea fishing excursions. I folded the papers and was placing them back on the stand when Griffin returned.

"Good news!" he exclaimed, "Marsha will take the day off if I get right over to her apartment. You gonna get work here?"

"I think we have to," I said. "We can't arrive in Cuba without a cushion of cash."

"I'll borrow some from Marsha," he said, "And by the way, she said there's a Salvation Army place on Flagler Street that has a good reputation. They also have job listings. You'll be fine."

I didn't respond.

He grabbed my shoulder. "I'm looking out for you, right?"

"Is that what you're doing?"

"Don't get weird on me, man."

"Marsha couldn't put me up too? Did you even ask her?"

"Look, man. That would be super awkward. We had something going, you know, and it still has serious energy for her. You understand that." He tore a corner off one of the newspapers and wrote something on it.

I nodded, trying to maintain a neutral expression. He signaled to an approaching cab. It swung over to the curb near us.

"Don't sweat it," he said. "It'll just be a couple of days. You'll be working. Here, this is the phone number. I'll call you later." He handed me the scrap of paper, clapped me on the back, and was gone.

As soon as the Salvation Army threw open its door at five o'clock I signed in along with a bunch of older men, most of them winos or guys clearly down on their luck. We were assigned steel bunks and told to clean ourselves up before prayer meeting. After a lengthy sermon on the perils of alcohol, we were ushered into an institutional dining room and given plates filled with a sort of tomato-flavored mush along with dry slices of rye bread. At ten o'clock the outer doors would be locked. That left us two free hours to watch television or play cards, or to go out. While most of the men went out, I stayed in, unwilling to risk missing a call from Griffin. For several hours I hung around the screen door, breathing in the rain-released odors and flicking my finger at insects hitting the screen. The drizzle finally ceased. The sun emerged just in time to sink from view in a haze of turquoise and purple streaks. Gradually the men began returning, shambling up the wooden steps, a few of them pausing to offer me a swig from bottles concealed in their shirts.

I was glad to burn off the lingering taste of supper with swallows of gin and rum. There was no phone call for me. I went to bed worried and slept badly.

Early the next morning I spent nearly half an hour with the chief officer of the place, Major Sykes. He handed me a postcard that had been mailed a few days earlier by someone wanting a house painted. After showing me where the house was on a pocket map, he let me use the house phone, assuring me my rucksack would be safe with him during the day. I phoned the number on the postcard, then called Griffin.

"It's an older couple," I told him. "They don't want to pay anything like union wages. They offered a dollar an hour and I'm gonna do it. I painted a house in Pittsburgh when I was in high school. This is the same sort of thing. She'll pay me at the end of each day."

"A buck an hour? In this heat? Christ Almighty."

"I know. I told her I could do it in four days, maybe five." I paused before adding curtly, "If you pitch in, we could finish in two or three days."

There was a long silence.

"I don't know how to paint houses," he finally said, "and besides, Marsha's going to lend us some cash."

"It's not hard," I protested. "I can show you."

"You eating okay?" he asked.

"Not bad. How are things with Martha?"

"It's Marsha. I wanted to talk to you about that. She's pretty well fixed. We had char-broiled steaks and daiquiris last night. She knows about our plans."

"I thought we agreed not to—"

"I promised to take her swimming this afternoon," he said.

"Don't rub it in. Do what you want. I need to be working."

He didn't respond.

"Will you be ready to leave by the time I'm finished with the house?"

"You sound pissed off."

I slammed the phone back on the receiver.

* * *

Four muggy and blisteringly hot days later, with the paint dry and gleaming on the house, I was ready to start on the trim. It was coolest in the early morning. I felt good as I pried the paint cans open with a screwdriver and stirred an experimental batch with a broken yardstick until the mixture looked to be the tint they wanted. I spread dropcloths over their exotic shrubs and walked back to the front porch as the couple was just putting golf bags into their car trunk. She was a heavyset woman wearing Bermuda shorts. Her husband wore a plaid jacket.

"That's quite a tan you're getting there," he said.

"I expect to finish today," I replied. "What time will you be back?"

"Today?" she piped up incredulously, "You'll finish today? What about the garage?"

"The garage? I thought you said just the house."

"And the birdhouse," she added. "Paint it the trim color, Paul. That'll be nice."

"Can you caddy?" Mr Abrams said. "You could take it easy today, just carry doubles for us, make some extra money."

"This has to be my last day here," I said. "If you're going to be back late, could you pay me now? It's thirty-eight dollars."

"You'll be cleaning up after you're done?" he asked, pulling out his wallet. I nodded and he handed me two twenty-dollar bills, then said, "Don't suppose you have two dollars on you?"

I ignored the question and they drove off.

Spurred by eagerness to finish, I worked even faster than the previous days. With the soreness nearly gone from both arms, I brushed on the trim color with decisive strokes, pausing only to move the ladder and wipe sweat from my eyes, or take a quick drink from the garden hose coiled in the garage. The sun poured down with increasing force. It was least bearable in the late afternoon. I could feel it penetrating my paint-stiffened shirt and burning into my skin. Several times I soaked my shirt and an old baseball cap by turning the hose onto myself full blast. The sun dried them both in minutes. By early evening I had a headache, and my eyes were stinging sharply from staring into that blazing white paint hour after hour. But at last the house was done, and the owners were not yet back. I returned the equipment to the garage and propped the brushes in a can of turpentine. The garage and the birdhouse remained unpainted. The house looked good.

Forty minutes later I got off one of the city buses and wearily traipsed the two blocks to the Salvation Army building. Griffin was sitting on the front steps, looking irritatingly cool and composed. He was dressed in fresh white slacks and a white shirt that intensified the dark tan on his arms and face. The relief I felt at seeing him was intense. He rose to his feet and we shook hands.

"I can smell the turpentine from here," he said. "Grab a shower and I'll buy us some daiquiris. You've carried this painting bullshit much too far, you look beat. You've got paint on your nose."

I rubbed a hand over my face.

"Missed it," he said. Plucking a clean handkerchief from his hip pocket, he daubed at the side of my nose, then held up the handkerchief so I could see the smudge.

"Where's Martha?" I asked.

"Marsha. She knows we're on a plane tomorrow. She's cool. I've interrupted her calendar enough as it is. Look, never mind that shower. We both could stand a drink."

"But I'll miss the meal here."

"Lucky you."

We set off walking. After several blocks I motioned toward a tavern across the street. "Not that dump," he said. "Let's find a hotel bar. I want to introduce you to a proper daiquiri." I remained silent.

"You still sore at me?" he said.

"Mostly just exhausted."

"A drink will fix that." Not much later we found ourselves inside an air-conditioned hotel bar with padded booths and no television.

"Pretty classy," I said, looking around. Think they'll let me stay here in these duds?"

"They won't care." We slid into a rear booth and I dropped the paint-spattered cap on the seat beside me. A waiter came over immediately and swirled a damp cloth over our table.

"A couple of daiquiris," Griffin said to him. "Each."

"ID please," the waiter said, looking at me suspiciously.

Griffin smoothed three one-dollar bills onto the moist surface of the table. "He's plenty old enough," he said. "Light on the sugar, heavy on the rum."

"Yes, sir," the waiter said, unobtrusively peeling the bills from the table. "Four daiquiris it is, sir."

Griffin leaned back and thoughtfully surveyed me.

The waiter set two little cardboard disks before each of us and placed a frosted pale green glass on each disk. He added a dish of salted peanuts and two cocktail napkins.

"Drink up," Griffin said jovially. I lifted my glass by the stem and watched Griffin clink the rim of it with his glass. "Here's to rebellion, *amigo*."

We both took long swallows that drained the shallow basins. It was my first daiquiri. I liked the sweet lime taste.

"By God," Griffin murmured. "This is a noble beverage. Like it?"

"It tastes expensive. I've only earned about $35. How much did you get from Marsha?"

"Enough to assure you that you've seen the last of slave labor. We're on a bus to Key West first thing in the *mañana*."

"Everything go okay with Marsha?"

"Not really. She's one of those young American mothers that are childless. Does that explain it?"

"Not exactly."

"She's the type that reads Doctor Spock and Edna St. Vincent Millay. She buys me all kinds of little things, mends my clothes, always wants to give me manicures or a haircut. She leaves little notes on the refrigerator—'Ricky, find roast chicken in casserole dish.' Then I find another note saying 'Hope you like it!' Little touches like that."

"You're talking about Martha?" I asked somewhat hazily.

The waiter wiped the wet rings and specks of salt off the table and set two fresh glasses on two new cardboard disks.

"Take this," Griffin called after him as he moved away. The waiter caught the empty peanut dish in midair.

A wave of well-being was enveloping me. "You find out anything about Cuba? About any underground? Any contact?"

"They hang out, these guys, in this bar in Miami proper," he said. "Marsha wanted to demonstrate how involved she was, so we went there. Pot-bellied guys wearing neckties with portraits of Castro. Women with enamel earrings that said 'Viva Fidel.' Cuban flags and banners all over the place."

"All right!" I said.

"So we got there and pushed through this mob of jabberers all trying to out-do one another. Sweaty guys all ages strutting around. We pushed through to this one fat guy in a booth. Marsha introduced us."

"He was the leader? Was he Cuban?"

"They were all Cuban. They go on maneuvers in the Everglades with air guns and switchblades. This guy invited me to join them. I asked him straight out why they didn't just go to Cuba and join Castro. Know what he said?"

"How could I?"

"He said it's impossible to get into Cuba right now. They're practicing with speedboats in the Everglades."

"You didn't tell him about us?"

"He did all the talking. Get a load of their plan. Batista, he told us, has tanks and artillery surrounding the Sierra

Maestra, which is where we're going, right? So these Florida characters want nothing to do with the mountains. They're planning an all-out assault directly on Havana."

"Think there's anything to it?" I asked.

"Think about it. It makes no sense. They're jerks."

Nodding sagely, I leaned back and studied my empty glass.

"That bother you?" he said.

"Does what bother me?"

"My calling them jerks."

"Why would it bother me?"

"It mightily annoyed Marsha," he said. "She gave me hell. She said, 'I'd like to see the day *you* get in there and fight a dictator.'"

"She really said that?"

"She did. And that was the end of our romance. But in a way we did have something together that was almost real. Let's have another round."

"We need to eat. Let's find some food."

"*Muy bien.* I'm personally going to have *langusto* and steak and a fudge sundae and—." He waved wildly for the waiter. "*Camarero!*" he shouted.

"After we eat, let's swim in the ocean," I said.

The waiter hurried over with a bill and Griffin handed him some cash. We slid out of the booth and walked toward the door, moving unsteadily yet very deliberately. A blast of heat hit us as we stepped out of the air conditioning. It was dark by then and the streets blazed with a thousand beckoning lights.

* * *

The clerk at the Cubana counter in the Key West Airport pushed two tickets and a few coins across the counter to Griffin.

"Checked baggage?"

"Just this," Griffin added, hoisting his bag, "but I'll keep it with me."

"And you?"

"Just this bag," I said.

"It will never get through," he said flatly.

"It won't?"

"Military articles are not permitted Cuban entry."

"But it's not a military article," I insisted.

"I can see that," he said with a smooth sort of officiousness. "But the fact remains, it looks like military issue."

"You should know," the clerk continued, "that just last week three fellows flew out of here and were sent back on the return flight because one of them was wearing an army fatigue jacket."

Griffin removed his dark glasses and dangled them from one finger. "So what do you suggest?" he asked.

"I suggest you get a suitcase."

"I'll keep it with me," I intervened. "And see what happens."

The clerk shrugged.

We carried the offending bag across the lobby to two vacant armchairs in a corner. We sat down and I hastily draped my legs over the rucksack. Griffin put on his sun-glasses.

"What did I tell you," he muttered. "Might as well be wearing Army surplus, for Christ's sake. We're transparent even to a clown like that."

"Think I should ditch this bag?"

"How do I know?"

I'd insisted we should pose as student campers, wearing bland clothes, although Griffin wasn't sure. We had on sport shirts and khaki slacks with little belts at the back. The cuffs of our slacks just barely covered the tops of combat boots we'd bought in an Army-Navy store an hour before leaving Miami.

"I don't know what makes you so certain we wouldn't sail straight through as journalists? We do have press passes," I said.

"Possibly because I have great difficulty believing we'll sail through at all."

"It's a damn sight better than what you came up with," I said. "Franciscan monks!" His idea for getting us past Cuban customs was to shave our heads, put on brown wool robes with rope belts and leather sandals, and stroll past the inspectors with folded hands and pious expressions.

He glanced around the lobby. "This is really classic," he snorted. "Do you even remember what students look like? There, those are students."

I turned and saw a group of four or five Americans standing at the counter, New Englanders probably, wearing an academic assortment of crew-cuts, horn-rimmed glasses, tweedy sport coats, and white buck shoes.

"The very image of what we're supposed to be," said Griffin, "red-blooded boys on semester break. The only difference is we look like beachcombers and they look like rich kids out to play some roulette. They won't even be checked."

"What makes you so sure they'll check us?"

"Don't worry," he said ominously, "they will."

"How about taking off those sinister glasses then," I said. "Talk about being obvious."

He frowned at me over the tops of them. "At least my plan had real beauty. You just lack the imagination to see it."

"Common sense prevails."

"No, it doesn't," he said with sudden sobriety. "Neither of us has an atom of common sense."

I ran a hand through my hair and glanced again at the clock. He sank deeper into his chair and re-crossed his legs. For a few minutes we drummed fingertips on the arms of our chairs until a loudspeaker abruptly crackled into action announcing our flight. I grabbed my bag, Griffin located our tickets, and we made our way through the lobby and out into the late afternoon heat on the landing field. A twin engine Cubana Airlines plane was warming up, its sleek fuselage a blinding silver in the sun. As we mounted the metal stairs, I noticed thousands of grasshoppers or locusts flipping around in the heat waves spanning the parched airfield. One of them ricocheted across my boot.

The stewardess examined our tickets and pointed us toward the middle of the plane. We maneuvered our bags down the narrow aisle and sank into our seats, not talking, just watching the other passengers settle in. A large party of Rotarians had boarded ahead of us. A lone nurse was helping a little Cuban girl with steel braces on her legs. The group of students boarded just after us, complaining about the heat and speculating about Cuban beer. They were followed by two elderly couples that had the look of returning Cubans. Last of all was a trio of Italian-American businessmen in elegant dark suits.

When we were all seated, the engines subsided for a brief lull before coughing into action and racing to a deafening roar, one that provoked in me a wild surge of excitement, a feeling of anticipation unlike anything I'd ever experienced. The desiccated airfield glided past outside the window, faster and faster until it was merely a brownish blur. And then we were airborne.

"What's the matter?" Griffin asked.

"Nothing."

"The way you're gripping my leg, I thought you might be—"

"Just excited I guess."

The plane climbed quickly. Within minutes we were suspended over water. Below us lay the magnificent sweep of the Caribbean, a sparkling bright turquoise here and there darkened by a violet patch of shadow or the dark green of an island. It was my first time flying and the aerial perspective was exhilarating. For a long time I gazed past the wing-tip down at the sea, thrilled by the incredibly tranquil look of everything from that height, awed at seeing clouds floating beneath us.

"Look at the way the sun hits the water!" I exclaimed.

Some twenty minutes into the flight the plane began to shudder.

"It's nothing," Griffin said. "Just turbulence."

The fasten seat belt sign blinked on. The elderly woman across the aisle from us snatched the paper bag from the pocket in front of her and leaned over it. A wave of nausea came over me. Hurriedly I focused the overhead air vent directly on my face and leaned back, eyes resolutely closed.

Then Griffin's elbow was prodding my ribs.

"Wake up," he said. "Behold the Pearl of the Antilles."

5

I could see, far below, the shadow of our plane gliding over the suburbs of Havana. It swept across thousands of flat roofs like pastel swatches among dark treetops.

"Scares you, doesn't it?" Griffin remarked, leaning over my legs to look down. "You can see every detail. Like those cars crawling along. Just think how hard it would be to hide from a plane. You wouldn't stand a chance."

The plane turned in a graceful arc, gradually descending. The seatbelt instructions were flashed again, and a moment later we were approaching a vast yellow field dotted with markers and crisscrossed with runways. The wheels bumped down in a series of jolts. We sped past numerous rows of fighter planes and vintage war planes, among them some sleek new jets and a number of bombers, blunt-nosed powerful jobs with wicked-looking wing cannons.

"The enemy," Griffin said. "Now's your chance, Paul. Jump out and start dismantling them."

"Unfunny."

"It's easy to see why your boy is having such a hard time," he said quietly. "Those are serious firepower."

"Why do you suppose they're not closer to the mountains?"

"No idea, but you needn't worry since we'll be back in Key West in another hour or so," Griffin said.

"Don't jinx us."

He laughed drily and a few minutes later held us back while the other passengers began filing out. As the collegians neared our seats, Griffin stepped into the aisle, neatly blocking them while I got down my rucksack and entered the flow. We walked out in their midst down rickety metal steps into dazzling sunlight. The passengers ahead of us wasted no time getting into the shade of the customs building while the students lingered to remove their jackets and sling them over their shoulders. Griffin paused too, kneeling to retie one of his bootlaces. We appeared to be part of their group as we moved across a dusty stretch of grass and entered a line just inside the building.

"Relax," Griffin murmured, "You look much too worried."

Inside it was dank and humid, and it seemed very dark after the light outside. I squinted to make out the official notices in Spanish all over the walls.

"What do they say?" I wondered aloud.

"Nothing," Griffin replied. "Got the visas?"

I nodded as the line moved slowly forward. We listened to the Ivy Leaguers' enviably casual chatter as we approached a metal table where a man in a khaki uniform sat sleepily scanning the visas thrust before him. When we reached him I held my visa up, and Griffin did the same. He motioned us on with a slight inclination of his head, and we followed the line into a second room.

"See? Nothing to it," Griffin said. "Like all officials, they don't give a damn." Neither of us believed that, but it was nice to hear as I surveyed the second room, a very large one with a concrete floor littered with cigarette butts. At one end was a long steel table behind which stood some dozen men in uniforms. All had guns in leather holsters strapped at their waists. They didn't look sleepy. Nor did the armed guard blocking the screened exit at the far end of the room.

He was a tall, muscular Negro cradling a submachine gun and looking us over as we found a space near the middle of the steel table.

I set down my rucksack and Griffin dropped his bag beside it.

The other passengers were dispersed along the table in two's and three's impatiently waiting to be tended. The three inspectors actually working were doing an impressively thorough job of opening one bag at a time, poking around in it, asking the owner a question or two, and finally jotting a cryptic mark on the bag with chalk. At that point the owner was free to step around the guard and go out the door. Finally an inspector stopped in front of my rucksack. Dark streaks of sweat stained the front of his shirt. I took a step forward to indicate the bag was mine, but he ignored this and went over to some other inspectors who were chatting among themselves.

"What's he–?" I began.

"Don't talk," Griffin said.

The other inspectors looked over at us. Stupidly enough, I began whistling. The inspector returned. Ignoring my rucksack, he opened the first of the collegians' four suitcases, pushed some shirts and underwear around, chalked a mark on the fabric, and unzipped the next suitcase.

"Stop whistling," Griffin said under his breath, glaring at me over his sunglasses. I stopped. Clearly, we were being kept for last. The nurse with the little crippled girl and the four students left together. As they were filing out through the screened exit, yet another uniformed guy pushed in past them and called out something in Spanish.

"Just a bus driver," Griffin said, "The last bus to Havana is leaving."

"How will we—"

"Be quiet," he said in a whisper. The exit guard resumed his stance blocking the doorway. We were the only ones still on our side of the steel table. We waited as the inspectors met in a quiet huddle. Two of them detached themselves and closed in around my rucksack. A pale man with a glossy black mustache and sergeant's stripes ostentatiously placed one hand on the bag. The wall clock ticked loudly.

"*¿Habla usted español?*" the sergeant said at last.

"No, sir," I replied. "Just English." My Spanish phrase book was helping.

"*¿Y usted?*" he asked Griffin.

Griffin looked blankly at me.

"He's asking if you speak Spanish," I explained.

"Not yet," Griffin said. "I hope to learn it."

"You are traveling together?" the sergeant asked. "You have identification?"

I reached for my wallet. Griffin pulled out a driver's license. A few other inspectors edged around us as the sergeant examined that and an old student card I gave him. He painstakingly copied something from each of them onto a pad, tore off the page and ambled over to a filing cabinet.

"What is it you plan to do in Cuba?" an inspector asked. He pronounced it *'Cooba'*.

"Just relaxation," Griffin said. "Hiking. We want to see if your beaches are as beautiful as the tourist brochures say."

"What beaches, *señor*, will you be going to?"

"Varadero," I said, drawing a startled look from Griffin.

"Of course, Varadero," the sergeant said. "*Muy linda, Varadero.*"

We smiled at one another.

"Empty this pack, señor," he said to me.

I pulled open the bag's drawstrings and lifted out handfuls of wadded clothes, a medicine kit, a pair of sneakers with ballpoint pens tucked inside, two blank notebooks, a comb, toothbrush, toothpaste, and my books. There was also a knife in a leather sheath.

The sergeant picked up the medicine kit. As the others pressed in for a closer look he strewed the contents over the table: iodine, gauze, adhesive tape, water-purifying pills, a tube of burn ointment.

"What do you do with this?"

"It's for camping."

He jabbed at the sheathed knife with the tip of his forefinger. "And this?"

"Also camping." Something was bothering him. He leafed through the notebooks.

"Look," Griffin spoke up with an air of strained patience, "How come we're being delayed like this?"

He was ignored. The sergeant held my rucksack upside down and ran his hand around inside it, carefully pinching the seams. Apparently satisfied, he set it on the floor on his side of the table and tossed into it the sheathed knife and all the medical items.

"Now you," he said to Griffin. "Your bag please."

Griffin pulled out rumpled clothing and toiletries, several packs of cigarillos and a flashlight.

The inspector added the cigarillos and flashlight to my rucksack.

"*Muy bien,*" he said. "Tomorrow both of you must apply to our office in Havana. You will be expected there when the office opens. Nine o'clock. *¿Entiende?*" He handed me a pamphlet and tapped his finger on the address printed on the bottom of it.

"Yes, sir," I said, feeling some relief.

"But why?" Griffin asked. "What about all those things you took?"

"They are temporarily confiscated. Retrieve them when you leave Cuba."

One of the inspectors handed me a large paper sack and motioned for me to hurry. I started cramming my stuff into the sack.

"What about the cigarillos?" Griffin asked. "And his rucksack?"

I couldn't tell whether this was his temper or an act. Either was alarming. At that moment a new group of tourists, all speaking Spanish, poured into the room and headed for the baggage area.

"You must go to our central office," the sergeant said to me, ignoring him. "Do you understand this?"

"Yes, sir," I said.

Griffin and I hastily thrust the remaining things into his bag.

Making a shooing gesture with both hands, the sergeant turned to look over the new arrivals. The big guard with the submachine gun stepped aside as I followed Griffin out the screened door. With studied casualness we walked to where two taxis were idling at the corner. A sharp tremor of relief struck the back of my knees with such force I nearly stumbled. Griffin took a deep breath and let it out with exaggerated slowness.

"I felt like a little boy," he said. "They had all power, and he knew it."

"Think he was giving us a break?" I asked. "Letting us go?"

"Beats me. "

"I'm guessing we won't be showing up at that address," I said.

"We damn well won't."

"So we'll soon be wanted men." The ensuing taxi ride into the heart of Havana triggered a certain amount of bewilderment in me. While I didn't expect to see tanks or bomb craters in the residential neighborhoods we passed through, I assumed there'd be some sign of urban warfare, some evidence that a revolution was underway. It was frustrating to find nothing of the sort. For all my avid squinting down dim alleys and whipping around to look at shouting children, I saw no trace of conflict, or of anything indicating the country was ruled by a dictator.

"Tell me something," Griffin said. "How did you come up with that Varadero response?"

"It's a resort near Havana, sort of on our route. Supposed to have gorgeous white sand."

"Very cool you knew that," he said.

I was genuinely touched by the compliment. "I spent serious time in New York studying maps, reading about this island."

"This weirdly quiet island." he said.

"Maybe it's siesta time," I suggested.

"This is not Mexico." He sighed noisily. "That bitter coffee smell takes me back to Puerto Rico, and the shabby look of the buildings. Back at customs I was struck by the smell of pomade, and people squabbling in Spanish. On the *avenida* back there . . . those carts filled with Caribbean fruits and vegetables. Ever since we got here, I've been noticing how so many things are strangely familiar."

The buildings, mostly of five or six storeys, were dilapidated, eroded over the years by humidity and unrelenting sunbake. Clothing fluttered from lines stretching from rusted wrought iron balconies. Some blocks of small shops came into view. We could see streams of pedestrians, older women in black dresses and young women in colorful scanty clothing, all selecting vegetables and fish from curbside tables or wheelbarrows. The air was pungent with fruit rot and tobacco smoke. The neighborhood we were passing through looked impoverished. Small groups of barefoot children were playing tag, roller-skating, shouting.

"Let's get out and look around," Griffin said, after many more blocks observing the city. I agreed. Griffin asked the driver about Varadero.

"But that's where they're expecting us to go," I protested, once we were on the sidewalk.

"I doubt they believed you," he said. "Or maybe they did. In any case, they won't be looking for us until we fail to show up tomorrow morning."

"Why did you want them to think you don't speak Spanish," I asked.

"The less people in uniforms know about us, the better," he replied.

We were in the middle of a large paved square with ponderous statues and clouds of pigeons swirling around government buildings. I noticed on the far side of the square an army jeep moving along slowly, canvas top flapping above the heads of four soldiers, all seated, rifles held erect between their legs.

"See that?" I asked excitedly.

"Look to the right of them."

"Where?" I lowered my voice.

"I'm not going to point, for Christ's sake. There, in the shadow of that building with all the flags."

Standing in the shade of the huge arched entrance to one of the buildings were eight or ten helmeted soldiers, all holding rifles. They were positioned behind an orderly pile of sandbags above which projected the dark barrel of what looked like a massive machine gun. I tried not to stare. We strode on more or less aimlessly away from the square into a district with attractive cafés and bars under huge shade trees. Sprawled on benches were derelicts of all ages and descriptions, amputees, a blind woman with opaque eyes. A little girl was squatting just off the sidewalk. A few folks were begging, but the passing parade of tourists and smartly dressed Cubans appeared to ignore them.

"Good thing we changed dollars in Miami," I observed.

Griffin nodded, clearly distracted.

We passed doorways draped with strings of colored beads or bottle caps. There were sidewalk displays of tourist souvenirs—stuffed alligators, maracas, seashells with 'Cuba' painted on them. I kept looking for some sign

84

of the rebellion, at the very least some graffiti or chalk scrawl on the walls.

"Griffin," I finally ventured, "Doesn't this feel like a movie with a faulty soundtrack?"

"It's the oppression," he said.

"Is that it?"

"Sometimes you absolutely floor me, Paul. What did you expect?"

"I expected more activity, maybe even some music. This *is* the tropics, even it it is a dictatorship. I don't know what to make of it. It just seems so subdued. Was it like this in Puerto Rico? Do you remember much from that part of your life?'

"1 do, *seguro que sí,* but you know, we lived in a small town. I only remember troops being there once. My mother kept us inside the house and away from the windows all day one day. Nothing happened. I think they were looking for someone."

Shallow puddles among the cobblestones were beginning to reflect the evening sky's luminous colors. Shop window lights were blinking on. More soldiers were appearing, usually in pairs moving slowly along the sidewalks, watching the pedestrians.

"You know," Griffin said, "I've been listening to the language. Cuban Spanish has a different sound than Puerto Rican Spanish. There's a whole different lilt to it."

"Wait here," he said. Ducking into a little tobacco shop, he spoke in Spanish to the proprietor, an elderly woman with a yellow headband, smoking a cigar. She began opening various drawers and bringing out cigars for him to sniff. He made quite a production of it, rolling each one judiciously between his fingers, asking drawn-out questions, nodding sagely at her responses. I waiting outside until he emerged with a handful of unwrapped cigars, already puffing on one, looking unbearably triumphant. I was about to remind him of a possible curfew, but he proceeded directly across the street and entered a sort of hardware shop. Minutes later he emerged with a green canvas bag, like a gym bag, and tossed it to me.

"Get rid of that sack," he said. "Think you're old enough to smoke some of the world's finest tobacco?"

"Great," I said, delighted with the gym bag, delighted with his giving it to me, one so much like his. While I transferred my clothing into it, he leaned contentedly against a wall.

"That fragrance of cheap pomade," he said. "So familiar from San Juan. You want music, listen long enough and you'll hear it, especially drumming, that Afro-Cuban beat coming right out of the pavement and the walls, vibrating straight into your bones. *Ay Charanga.*"

Three older women rustled past us, darting suspicious glances.

"We can afford a hotel," he said. "A cheap hotel. We could see a bit of the nightlife. It's supposed to be fantastic."

"We need to save our money," I argued. "Besides that, we need to get the hell out of here. When we don't show up at their office, they'll probably put out a bulletin for our arrest. Let's not still be here."

"You don't care about seeing more of Havana?"

I shook my head emphatically. He crossed the street to where a Chinese youngster was standing in a doorway. After a moment, the kid pointed in the direction we'd been going. I hurried over to them.

"We may be stuck here," Griffin explained. "There are travel restrictions, probably roadblocks. We should check the trains and buses."

"Let's not screw around until we're the only people left on the street," I said.

"Right," he said. "They may already be scouring the whole damn countryside for you."

"And for you," I insisted.

"They have no idea who I am."

Startled, I stopped to stare at him.

"Don't just stand there," he said. "The train station is just a few more blocks."

"What do you mean, they don't know who you are? You gave them your driver's license."

"You continue thinking I'm an imbecile," he snapped.

"Well, what *did* you give them?"

"Never mind. Just try to understand that my leaving Havana with you is purely unselfish on my part. You're now a wanted man, Mr Paul Bell."

He continued to refuse to tell me whose license he had given them, or how he'd obtained it. I stopped asking, yet couldn't help feeling less assured of our friendship. They had my name. He was anonymous. It was annoying.

At least a dozen heavily armed soldiers were inside the railroad station, openly scrutinizing arrivals and departures. They didn't seem to be bothering anybody, but their presence was intimidating.

"Relax," Griffin said. "They're not interested in us. They have genuine armed revolutionaries to worry about. And by the way, I did try to get an ID for you. It didn't work out."

"You might have mentioned that," I said, instantly hating the sour tone in my voice.

"Tell me what you know about Varadero," he said.

"I'm guessing Americans don't stand out there," I said. "And it's on our way south, not far from Matanzas."

"Know anything about Matanzas?" Griffin asked.

"Nope."

"So much for your study of Cuban geography."

"About which you know even less."

Although he was hesitant, we went ahead and got tickets to Matanzas. To kill the hour before departure and to escape military surveillance near the station, we went to a café we'd seen on our way there—a seedy little joint that smelled of rancid cooking oil. We flopped onto plastic chairs at a cracked plastic table near the front window and Griffin ordered us each a *café con leche* while I looked around. Scotch-taped to the walls were discolored pictures torn from magazines—Marilyn Monroe, Bridget Bardot, Jane Russell. There was a limp pennant commemorating the long-gone St Louis Browns. Over everything was a heavy film of grease. Under the corner tables I noticed rat-traps baited with morsels of molding bread.

"I'm tired," Griffin said, as an espresso machine sputtered into action. "I didn't feel it until we sat down, but I'm bushed."

"Maybe we'll get some sleep on the train."

"Don't count on it. I'm still wondering if maybe we should stay here a while longer, get the feel of things, maybe make some contact with the underground. As it is, we're plunging headlong into the countryside. It worries me that you're such an incredibly conspicuous Anglo."

"Well, that's not going to change, is it?" I snapped, more sharply than I meant to. "Anyway, we have our tickets."

He slumped down in his chair and began wearily beating out on the rim of the table an accompaniment to the Afro-Cuban strains coming from the jukebox of a larger café across the street.

The proprietor brought our coffee and a little plate containing two cubes of sugar wrapped in soiled paper. We peeled them, stirred them into the thick liquid and sipped.

"You know," I said, "it's not good to get so worn out. We start bickering and the whole project begins to seem insane."

"I know what you mean." We sipped again and gazed out the window.

"This is *real* coffee," he said, "not that Yankee slop you like. I love this coffee."

His eyes were closed. "I remember it from childhood. My mother made coffee just like this. It's the real thing, the dark blood of the earth itself."

"The dark blood of the earth itself with steamed milk," I said drily.

"Maybe you have to have Spanish blood," he countered. "Maybe that's why I've always felt like an outsider in your country. I never fit in with you Anglo-Saxons."

"Me neither," I said. "I never fit in with us Anglo-Saxons either."

He scowled at me.

"Oh, go ahead," I said, "just call me *gringo*. I know you want to."

"Yeah, well, it's in the blood."

"Of course, Herr Hitler. Come off it."

"Believe what you want," he said, smiling faintly. "I'm telling you, it's all coming back."

"Where's the toilet in this dump? or don't they have such Anglo-Saxon niceties?"

"Right over there, the door marked *caballeros*."

When I returned to the table a moment later, Griffin scraped back his chair and headed for the same place. I turned to watch the people on the street. The sun was setting, turning that orange tone to a purple twilight between the buildings. It had cooled off enough for there to be a steady procession of couples out for a breath of air. We still didn't know if there was a curfew in effect.

* * *

The train seats were worn wooden ones in an overcrowded car full of country people, *campesinos,* and their animals. They littered the aisle, filled seats, and stuffed the overhead baggage racks—roosters in crude wooden crates, baby pigs stuffed into hampers or held tightly in laps. This astonished me. Griffin wasn't fazed. In fact, he was pleased, predicting the *campesinos* would soon be passing around bread and cheese and wine, as he claimed poor farmers habitually did on European trains. He went on to say there would likely be guitars brought out, plus good-natured jokes and ribald Cuban songs. None of this happened. We were under the sullen surveillance of soldiers with machineguns, one posted in the front of the car, one in the rear. There was nothing to be seen in the dense blackness outside the windows, although most of the *campesinos* stayed awake, eyes obstinately staring outside, mouths clamped shut.

Possibly it was a form of protest against the soldiers but I doubted it. They seemed to be cowed, resigned to meager lives of poverty and humiliation. I didn't want to stare at them, yet it was impossible not to notice how under-nourished and grim they were, their faces pinched with overwork and often pocked with disease. The jerky motion of the train had their bodies jiggling like so much abject gristle while their animals kept up a wild barnyard clamor.

Periodic lurches sent crates skidding along the aisle and baskets tumbling down from the racks. Geese and roosters squawked and tried to beat cramped wings. Pigs let out high-pitched squeals. Soon the car was reeking of urine and the overpowering stench of animals disoriented and defecating. To make matters even worse, the car was soon overheated, and there were no open windows. Griffin leaned his head against my shoulder and fell asleep, while I contined to study the people around us. So many were physically damaged, even the young ones, some with filthy bare feet mottled with open sores.

At last the train screeched to a stop. A solitary light bulb revealed the word *Matanzas* painted on a dark station house. There were no indications of a town. Beyond the yellow squares of light falling from the train windows onto the platform, illumining the trees and deep grass on both sides, everything was dark. The air had a peculiar sweet smell and was wonderfully fresh. We drank in deep breaths of it while watching a number of the *campesinos* climb off the train, shouldering their possessions. The minute they touched the platform, after a quick glance at us, they moved off into the night, disappearing into humid darkness. We listened to the sounds of their animals getting farther and farther away.

"Know what it means?" Griffin asked. "Matanzas?"

"Nope."

"Massacres, killings," he said. "But that pineapple certainly smells delicious."

With his boots clomping on the wooden planks and mine sounding an accompaniment, we made our way to the end of the platform and jumped to the ground. A dirt path led into a dark thicket of trees.

"Where are we going?" I asked.

"This has to lead somewhere. If it doesn't, we'll try the other way."

We were pushing branches and twigs away from our faces when two figures suddenly appeared on the path just ahead of us. Hearing a distinctly metallic and ominous *click-click,* we froze in our tracks.

"Varadero," Griffin called out. "*¿Dónde está Varadero?*"

No response. I had an urge to bolt but Griffin moved cautiously forward and I remained at his side.

We advanced enough to see two men in dark uniforms—local police, I guessed. Another stride revealed the drawn pistol held by one of them, and by then we could see they were both fairly old and paunchy, probably unnerved to be confronting us.

"*Buenas tardes, señores,*" Griffin said amicably. "*¿Por favor, dónde está Varadero?*"

The one with the pistol fumbled it into his holster then abruptly pulled it out again.

"*Buenas noches,*" the other one said. "*¿Norteamericanos?*" He wore thick glasses and looked nervous.

"*Sí, sí, americanos,*" we both said in unison.

Apparently bewildered that two young foreigners had appeared at this hour on their beat, they went into whispered consultation. The one with the pistol again holstered it.

"Can you understand what they're saying?" I asked Griffin.

Their conversation ceased and they both stared at me with expressions of stupefaction, as though they'd never heard another language spoken.

"*Por favor,*" Griffin said again, "*¿Varadero?*"

One of them sternly ordered us to follow them. They led us through the trees back to the station house. In the front of it was an unpaved road, lit only by faint moonlight. They paused and pointed triumphantly up the road toward the dark outline of a hill.

"*Mira ahora, americanos,*" said one of them. "*Ma-tan-zas.*" He jabbed his pointed finger in that direction for a good ten seconds before turning around and jabbing his finger in the opposite direction.

"*Mira,*" he said slowly. "*Va-ra-de-ro.*"

"They think we're imbeciles," I guessed aloud.

"They're right," Griffin said. He thanked them, and we watched them head back into the woods before we began hiking in the specified direction. There were no lights, no buildings, just the musky darkness of pineapple fields stretching on and on, an ideal place for walking fast. Well before dawn we left the road, stretched out in a field and almost immediately fell asleep on the damp earth.

* * *

I'd never seen a landscape as purely beautiful as Varadero Beach. The map showed it on Cuba's northern coast, a ten mile-long isthmus of stunning white sand that curled south into the Atlantic Ocean. Dark green palm trees and healthy palmettoes grew in scattered clusters between small houses and apartment buildings painted in a range of pastel colors. Varadero was touted as a world-famous tourist attraction, yet the area seemed surprisingly undeveloped. We walked along a deserted golf course built in the Twenties by the US financier DuPont, according to a signboard in English. Our hands and cheeks were still sticky with the juice of purloined pineapple. Despite being gritty, irritated, and sweating heavily, we proceeded straight on past the hotels, bars, and shops, all shuttered beneath faded awnings, all hushed in the clear morning light. The fruit-drink stands were also shuttered. We were happy to come across a motorized cart run by an old woman selling colas and cheese sandwiches. Behind her cart was a pile of green coconuts. We watched her deftly lop off their tops with a machete. For a few coins we could drink fresh coconut milk. The exchange rate for dollars was so good it surprised us how little things cost. We thirstily drained a coconut each. For a few coins more she sloshed out some of the milk, replaced it with rum, lime juice, and sugar, then shook the coconut vigorously. Carrying one each, sipping through straws, we strolled on, disheveled but definitely relaxing.

"Just wait until the sun goes down," Griffin said. "This place will be jumping. What we need now is a swim," he proposed, "something to clear our heads, so we can plan our next move."

"Still thinking we should hitchhike?"

"Probably not," he replied, "I'm not sure."

We were both undergoing a mildly disquieting premonition about lingering in Varadero, at the same becoming a little goofy with the rum, when I suddenly broke out laughing. Then Griffin started laughing as well. We seemed to have the entire place to ourselves. We sauntered past a few hotels along a dusty lane that stretched between fields studded with rows of spiky henequen plants, palm trees, and flowery pink bushes, until finally we arrived at the beach, the sea luminous in the near distance. By then the sun was spread across the sky like liquid white metal. The only audible sound was the drone of insects accompanied by the lapping of gentle waves washing in from a turquoise sea. The beach was a long expanse of unblemished sand, nearly a pure white. Without slowing down or saying a word, we tramped over it, dropped our bags, pulled off our shoes, and waded straight into the water up to our waists before simultaneously crashing through the surface with head-first plunges. The water was so clear we could see crabs scuttling on the bottom, and fish moving languidly, casting shadows on the sandy floor. We floated on our backs, still clothed, pleasantly buoyed by the balloons of air trapped in our shirt and trousers. When at last we left the water, we spread our clothes out to dry in the sun and lay down to sleep in the shade at the edge of the beach. Another hour must have passed before we heard the distant cries of children playing in the surf. We could see a few beach umbrellas, and a number of people sitting around them. We got dressed, brushed off the sand, fingered our hair into something like neatness, and began walking back to the road.

"I have an idea that might help us stay out of trouble," I said.

"I need another one of those coconut drinks," he replied.

"Guantánamo," I kept on. "It's an American base on the far side of the Sierra Maestra. Think about it. If we run into complications we can just say we're going there to visit relatives or something. Gives us a reason to be here."

"Why can't they have the revolution right here in Varadero?" Griffin asked.

"We need to check the bus schedule," I said, "See what our options are."

"Don't tell me," he persisted. "It's because they're communists. Communists hate pleasure, right?"

We bought sunglasses and cheap *sombreros* with ragged fringes at a little shop for tourists before boarding, around noon, the only bus to Santa Clara. It was parked on the street, with two wheels drawn up onto the sidewalk. Smaller than a school bus, it had bits of straw projecting from the many grease spots and splotches scattered among the dents that constituted its body.

The driver of this relic was an extremely wizened man who looked as old and contrary and battered as his vehicle. Finaly we were ready to start. The old bus put on a shuddering, gearstripping burst of acceleration, and we were on our way. Although the bus stayed on the central highway, it turned out to be a local run, picking up or dropping off *campesinos*—country people, their skin exceptionally weathered by the tropical sun. One couple boarded with a large rooster that settled onto the woman's lap. Griffin asked what the rooster's name was.

"Gallo," the man said curtly. *"Solamente gallo. Nada más."*

"Rooster," Griffin explained to me. "The bird's name is Rooster. His owner seems to think I'm weird for asking. By the way, how much Spanish are you understanding?"

"Very little," I said, "It's spoken so fast I'm getting almost nothing."

"Keep trying. It's difficult for me to get into any meaningful conversation when I have to keep interrupting to translate for you."

"Maybe," I suggested, "you could have your meaningful conversations and give me the gist afterwards."

"We'll see."

Irked a bit, I turned to the woman and pointed at an orchard of fruit trees we were passing.

"Señora," I said, *"por favor, cómo se llaman estos?"*

"Árboles," she replied. *"Sí, señor, árboles."*

"*Muchas gracias,*" I said, nodding vigorously.

Griffin chuckled.

"Okay," I muttered, "so what did she say?"

"She said those are trees. *Árboles.*" He smiled at the woman.

"Well, that's exactly what I wanted to know," I said.

"No, it's not," Griffin said. "You wanted to know what kind of trees they are. They're *guayabos.*"

"Oh," I nodded.

"*Guayabos,*" he repeated. "Guavas."

6

March, 1958

It was already afternoon when the bus lurched into the central bus station in Santa Clara. It parked directly across the street from two military tanks and about a dozen soldiers wearing camouflage, talking among themselves. A few of them looked in our direction as we got off the bus.

"The next town we're going to," Griffin said, "what is it?"

On the bus I'd been studying our map.

"Next is Ciego de Ávila. Then Camagüey."

"How far to the mountains?"

"The Sierra Maestra? Maybe five hundred miles."

"I guess hitching's out," Griffin said. "Nothing but military on the road. Let's get tickets."

Inside the station there were two clerks at the counter, one of them probably the father of the other. The older one patiently explained to Griffin that the bus no longer went any farther south than Camagüey. That was now the end of the line. He advised us to take the train if we wanted to go to Oriente Province, but there was a problem with the train. Both clerks firmly agreed there was a problem. They wouldn't say more. The next bus was scheduled to leave in three hours, at seven o'clock. I was looking at the map when the older clerk abruptly plucked a straw hat from a wall hook, said something to the younger guy and walked out, letting the screen door slam behimd him.

"You go Guantánamo?" the younger clerk asked, "You are *yanqui* sailors?"

"No," I said. "We're not sailors."

"You are *yanquis, pero* . . . not sailors?" he persisted.

I nodded. He seemed mystified.

"You don't go Guantánamo?"

"Why are you asking?" Griffin spoke up.

The clerk looked from him back to me. "You are *yanquis*, you go Oriente Province," he said, clearly bothered by this.

"We are journalists," I said. *"Periodistas."*

Griffin winced.

A woman holding a baby, trying to conceal her nursing, pushed her way in through the door. The clerk greeted her politely, then took my map and used a red pencil to circle on it the name of a town.

"Bayamo?" I asked.

"Sí, sí, my cousin is there," he replied, voice lowered, now mildly distressed, "He is Gerardo. Gerardo at Café Bayamo. You go there," he said. "Two tickets, seven o'clock."

Griffin handed him some peso notes. The young clerk gave him the tickets with some coins before turning to the woman.

"Buenos días, señora," he said brightly.

Back on the street, the tanks and soldiers hadn't moved. We walked away from them, not talking until we'd turned the corner.

"What was that about?" I asked.

"It was perplexing," Griffin said. "Very odd. Gerardo might actually be a contact, but Paul, you just put us at risk. You can't tell people we're journalists. It's like saying we support Castro. You think those soldiers wouldn't like to know that? They'd be more than happy to interrogate us. Let me be the one to figure out exactly who we should and shouldn't talk to, okay? Promise me that."

"I had a sense this guy was okay, that he wasn't any danger."

"You had a sense," Griffin said sardonically. "Please don't have that sense again. Anyway, I'm hungry. Let's find a place to eat."

After several beers with plates of tasty rice, beans, and chicken in a little café, I felt a lot better. Possibly I had made a mistake, but we now we had the name of a possible contact. Finding a park bench in some shade, we sat down and soon dozed off in the heat.

At seven o'clock we were back on the bus going south, with a sack containing olives, bread rolls, and a bottle of rum. Soon we were rolling down the *Carretera Central* of Cuba, an impressive name for a two-lane strip of deteriorated concrete splitting a vast stretch of grassy plains, tobacco and sugar fields, mango orchards, and low, wooded hills, almost the length of Cuba. The highway was basically unlit. There were no guard rails or glass reflectors. As night fell, the sole illumination was the headlights. Scattered every few miles were unlit or dimly-lit dwellings, often in groves of dark trees. We passed a few gas stations, but all were closed. There was extremely little traffic. Mile after dark mile we hurtled down the country's major thoroughfare without encountering another vehicle.

Finally the bus stopped in a rural town to pick up more passengers, as well as two hogs, a baby donkey, a parrot in a bamboo cage, and a fat guy carrying a heavily-worn leather saddle. The driver waited until all were settled toward the back, hogs hoisted onto separate seats and roped down, the donkey tethered in the aisle in the very rear. As we pulled away from the few town lights, plunging into the dark again, the bus picked up speed. The couple seated behind the pigs reached over the seat and tried to quiet the noisy one. Soon the interior began smelling awful.

"This is unreal," I said to Griffin, laughing. "We're in a Cuban Noah's Ark."

He handed me the pint bottle of rum and a few black olives. "Welcome to the third world."

I'd never tasted rum. After a few welcome swigs, I checked the windows. I'd assumed they were fixed glass panes, the knobs merely decorative, but I saw they could be opened. I yanked down hard on the one by my seat. It opened a few inches. When I yanked down on it again, there was an outburst of shouting from the front, and a soldier I hadn't noticed was rushing up the aisle toward me, his rifle raised, shouting something I couldn't understand. Hurriedly I handed Griffin the bottle and raised my hands into the surrender position.

"Sit down," Griffin barked at me. "No open windows!"

"Hell no," I said. "I'm sick of this stink."

He grabbed my belt and wrenched me back down into the seat, just as the soldier slammed the butt of his rifle into my chest with such force I nearly passed out. Then he turned his weapon around and jabbed the muzzle into my shirt directly above my heart. The other riders ignored all this, except for the parrot, which began making blood-curdling shrieks.

"¡Identidad!" the soldier shouted. He was a teenager, maybe sixteen, with mixed blood and a heavily freckled face. I fumbled my wallet out and held up my old student ID card.

"Usted también," he shouted at Griffin, who immediately obeyed.

The bus driver was now there as well, glancing over the soldier's arm at our cards before tapping his wristwatch and saying something apparently persuasive to the soldier. Only then did the soldier click the safety on his rifle and swing the muzzle away from my chest. He handed us back our IDs but kept standing in the aisle next to me.

I let out a long breath.

"Anything broken?" Griffin asked with real concern.

I felt to see if a rib had been broken. Griffin rushed to explain in Spanish, with excessive politeness, that I was an American tourist—a very stupid one, he emphasized, even for a *yanqui*, and that I couldn't speak Spanish so couldn't possibly understand the very clear and sensible rule the soldier was enforcing. Only slightly mollified, the soldier made his way back to the front of the bus. My chest really hurt. Normal breathing had resumed somewhat raggedly. Griffin took the opportunity at that point to translate for me his own diplomatic eloquence in my defense.

"That can't be legal," I protested, still feeling the shock. "Bashing a foreigner with a rifle?"

"You need to understand," Griffin leaned close to my ear, "there's no law here."

"But why the hell is there an order to keep the windows shut?"

"You really are an innocent," he said, "an American innocent. You make these ignorant Yankee presumptions. What did I just tell you? You still don't understand how something impulsive like that could get us both killed."

"Okay, okay," I protested, "I just wanted some fresh air."

"Don't presume that being American protects you," he went on, whispering hoarsely, "You think it does, but it doesn't. It's stupid and it's dangerous and I really do not want to die here. Or be tortured. Don't do *anything* to call attention to us. Do not mention the word *periodista,* the only word you seem to know in Spanish, and never, ever, mention Fidel or *26 de Julio.* Do you understand me?"

I nodded sheepishly. Griffin stood up, stretched, and went to sit a few seats behind me. Still very shaken, I thought it over and knew he was right. After that I kept a silent vigil out the window. My eyes gradually adjusted sufficiently to the dark to make out shapes faintly illuminated by moonlight, but I realized there was a considerable drawback to rushing headlong through everything at night.

Finally there appeared in the distance the dim lights of Ciego de Ávila, with lots of railroad tracks to go banging over. When the clatter of our engine subsided to a hoarse idling I could hear Griffin spitting olive pits onto the floor behind me and taking occasional slugs from his bottle.

We stopped just long enough to take on one more passenger—a stocky, frizzle-haired, middleaged guy who climbed aboard with a rope-tied suitcase. Instead of sitting in front with the others, he limped back toward us, pausing near me with an odd sort of questioning expression. He proceeded to the rear of the bus.

From there we rattled on for hours through unrelieved darkness. Scattered every few miles along the way were unlit thatched huts and small farms, illumined in the brief spray of headlights. It was an eerie sensation, traveling mile after dark mile through the center of the country without meeting any other vehicles. It was unnerving. If night traffic had been banned—the only explanation that occurred to me—I couldn't understand why our bus was still running. I'm not sure how much time passed before headlights appeared and flicked past us, a caravan of six jeeps racing in the opposite direction. Minutes later came three military trucks that sent our bus swerving onto the rough edge of the road. As they thundered northward after the jeeps I noticed each of them was canvas-rigged and bristling with armed soldiers.

"Hey, Griffin," I whispered, whirling around. "Did you see—"

I'd forgotten the newcomer, but there he was, sitting next to Griffin, staring blankly at me over the top of the Bacardi bottle. If he understood English there was no hint of it on his face. I resumed looking out the window, not sitting up until we rolled into the murkiness of a bus depot. The interior lights came on, allowing me to see the other passengers. In the seat directly across the aisle there was a young woman who had cataracts on both her eyes. They were a glazed a viscous blue-white. The guy with the saddle mounted on his lap had a withered arm and bare feet streaked with thick smears of what looked like dried blood. I stopped feeling sorry for myself, although my chest was still hurting, and began understanding why the only protests of the assault on me had come from animals. Griffin edged past me in the aisle followed by the guy with the roped suitcase.

"Twenty minute break," he said without pausing. "Don't get lost."

"Griffin?"

"What?"

"Nothing, never mind."

The frizzle-haired guy was right behind him, again giving me a peculiar look. I didn't like it. I followed them off the bus, keeping a distance. Three policemen reinforced by several armed soldiers were interrogating some of the passengers. Directly across the road were two military tanks and half a dozen other soldiers standing around talking among themselves under a string of red lights and lanterns. A few were looking in our direction, watching the passengers pull the donkey and hogs off the bus, then disappear into the darkness. The feared interrogation turned out to be simply a matter of showing ID. A soldier, an older guy with broken brown teeth, said something I didn't understand.

"¿Americano?" he asked.

"Americano, sí," I assured him.

"Bueno. No hay problema," he said.

The bus depot was a cavernous building with an oil-spattered concrete floor, more like a maintenance garage than a bus terminal. I used the station toilet and stretched my legs. I saw Griffin in the open doorway, completing a handshake with his companion and still talking. I waited, examining the ceiling and marvelling at the size of the insects circling the bare light bulbs overhead. Finally Griffin joined me.

"I learned a bit," he said softly. "For example, last night a limousine was blown to bits not far from here with a couple of local politicans in it."

"He wasn't a cop, was he?"

"That guy, no. He's a petty tax collector, something like that. He travels all over the country. He says we were lucky to get on this bus—they'll soon be cutting the service both ways, trying to close off the whole eastern province."

"You didn't—" I began apprehensively.

"Of course not. I told him we're going to Guantánamo, your bright idea. He believed it."

"What else did he say?"

"Nothing much," he said.

"You don't want to tell me?"

"It's ugly, Paul, what's going on. You don't want to know."

"I do want to know."

"You save any food for me?"

I told him there were a few olives. We walked back to where the bus was being refueled at an indoor pump. The soldiers and policemen had drifted off to distant corners of the depot to smoke away from the fumes. Very few passengers were returning to their seats. Only two new people boarded, a young couple who were slumped together across the aisle from my seat. I grabbed my bag and joined Griffin in the rear.

"No more rum," he said.

"You drank that whole bottle? Just the two of you?"

"I left it on the floor. One of the soldiers must have grabbed it."

He peered outside at the men in uniforms as the bus engine kicked into action with a loud reverberation that interrupted our conversation. Then we were back on the highway.

"What did your friend have to say about the rebels?" I asked.

"Nothing very important."

With that, we fell silent. By turns we stretched out across the long back seat and tried to get brief naps, but each attempt ended with sitting up and staring morosely out the window. Going through the next town we didn't even slow down. Crude irrigation ditches and pools of moonlit water began to appear as the miles passed. Gradually the entire countryside seemed to be taking on a wilder aspect—trees flashing by in the headlights, tangled reaches of marshland.

It was a relief to pull at last into Camagüey. A Coca-Cola sign popped into view, and a lighted billboard. Multiple-storey buildings appeared. Intersections became lit and paved. We halted in front of the bus station just long enough for the young couple to get off. No one got on. Only the staunch little driver and the young soldier remained aboard with Griffin and me as the bus surged forward yet again.

A few miles later a sudden cloudburst brought our bus to a halt, right there on the road. Rain smashed down on the roof with astonishing tropical force for maybe ten minutes before abruptly ceasing, leaving everything around us sodden and dripping. Only then did the bus continue along the central highway. Some time after that I looked up from my notebook, I'd been jotting things down, and saw a lighted billboard. Scrawled across the bottom in black paint were the words—*Viva 26 de Julio*. I nudged Griffin excitedly. He looked just in time to see it.

"Be cool," he whispered. "You never know who might be watching. And by the way, that's the second graffiti I've seen."

"Really? When was the other one?"

He just looked at me with an infuriating grin.

The next time the bus came to a stop I could only see dismal swampland. The bus door swung open and two soldiers cradling sub-machineguns stepped aboard and ordered us off the bus.

After an indifferent glance at us as we moved past them, they began shining flashlights under the seats. The air outside was misty, full of pre-dawn vapors rising from the swamp. A number of lighted lanterns were dangling from wooden sawhorses set across the highway a few yards ahead of the bus. More soldiers were impassively watching from the other side of the roadblock. On our side was a squat, heavily sandbagged structure surrounded by rolls of barbed wire. Behind it was yet another soldier seated behind the heaviest machinegun I'd ever seen.

"Just be calm," Griffin murmured, handing me my bag. "Tell them you lost your wallet in Varadero."

"I can handle myself," I said, testily.

I could hear little splashes in the swamp. An officer stepped forward and ordered us into a dirt-floored military tent lit by a kerosene lamp. There was a desk with a telephone and two piles of glossy photographs.

"Please remove your clothes," the officer said in English. Something in his manner suggested he disliked having to do this. He smiled genially, seeing Griffin unbuttoning his shirt with his gaze straight ahead, hands moving methodically. As we took off each item of clothing and laid it on the bare corner of the desk, the officer carefully scrutinized us. He and one of the soldiers never took their eyes off us or made a sound until we had both shed our underwear.

"Shoes," the officer said.

We knelt down and Griffin unlaced his boots while I did the same. The dirt floor was damp as we pulled off our socks and stood barefoot. The officer pointed at the wall behind us and ordered us to stand against it. Buck-naked and shivering, we backed up until we were standing against a dank wall of sandbags. Not once did we look at one another. Our eyes stayed on the officer. One of the soldiers inspected our clothing, shaking them out piece by piece before letting them drop to the floor. Then he went through our wallets and our bags with the same methodical deliberation. We watched with suppressed alarm, arms clasped over our chests. I didn't think we had anything incriminating, but I wasn't fully certain.

"Nada, teniente, no hay nada," the soldier reported at last.

The lieutenant seemed neither disappointed nor surprised. Calmly running a hand through his cropped grey hair, he murmured something and crossed the floor to take a stance directly in front of me. I couldn't move back. Damp sandbags were against my buttocks.

"Do you like Fidel Castro?" he asked, speaking a highly accented English. His brown eyes coolly stared into mine so closely I could smell his after-shave lotion.

"Fidel Castro," he repeated. " You like him?"

I cleared my throat. "I don't know. Is that a place? A town?"

He expression didn't change even slightly. He stared at each of us, said something to Griffin I couldn't hear, then turned away.

"Thank you for cooperation," he said. "You're free to go."

Our clothes went on much faster than they came off. I could hear the pre-dawn cries of birds. The sawhorses had been dragged off to the sides of the road, and the jeepload of soldiers was gone. The bus was still sitting in the middle of the road.

It must have been at least an hour later when I awoke to find the bus plowing with difficulty through a massive expanse of brown water extending across the highway and into the fields on each side. The bus managed to get across this flooded area and was negotiating a long grade, when I saw an explosive flurry of dark birds—crows or ravens—

flapping wildly around a telephone pole next to the highway. Perhaps a dozen of them in mid-air were tearing off bits of flesh from the remains of a naked human body hanging on the pole about eight feet off the ground. I shook Griffin awake, but by the time he was sufficiently roused, we were past it. A few miles later there was a similar scene that we both noticed at the same time. This one was clearly a young woman with long black hair and without clothes. She had a horribly twisted neck. She was wired to a utility pole. It looked as though small animals or large insects had eaten at her body nearly to the waist. It was sickening.

"Like a crucifixion," I said, deeply shocked.

"A warning," Griffin said grimly.

"Warning? She was a captured rebel?"

"Could be," he said. "Or a sympathizer. You know, like us."

"Let's hope we've got enough cash to actually get us to wherever the other side is."

Griffin smacked my leg, "You're in luck," he said. "We're already there."

We fell silent, preoccupied with our own thoughts, still intently scanning both sides of the highway. I was trying to dispel a kind of heavy fear centered in my chest, as though it were full of wet clay. Maybe it was only the bruise from the rifle butt, but my whole body had taken on a weighty numbness and pervasive dread I'd never felt before.

Not much later there appeared ahead of us in the watery dawn light, the immense pale violet peaks of what had to be the Sierra Maestra. We were finally in Oriente Province, where Fidel Castro had been born and where, less than two years ago, he had recklessly landed with some eighty-two other guys in a boat they called *Granma*. I read about this in New York. Most of them were immediately killed or captured by Batista's forces. The few survivors had climbed through swamps and rugged terrain to make a camp somewhere high in this very mountain range. Now, for

Fidel and his *26 de Julio* movement, it was the base for waging a civil war. I forced myself to suppress a tremendous surge of excitement. We were finally getting close.

7

Later in March, 1958, Bayamo

Bayamo was exactly the sort of town I'd expected to find in
Cuba. Street after unpaved street of open air market stalls
with throngs of people and panting dogs, bicycle riders and
horse riders and donkeys. There were groups of soldiers as
well, all carrying rifles, evidently on informal patrol,
ambling and observing, not bothering anybody. Near the
center of town we were borne along with the crowd of
shoppers, past stall after stall of fruits and vegetables, most
of them exotic and unknown to me. There were table-loads
of fish on melting ice, dripping carcasses of skinned pigs,
whole cows hanging upside down. One table held large,
headless turtles laying in their own blood. Fat black flies,
small green flies and various bees buzzed in swarms over
all the ripe fruit and displays of meat. Our sweat also
seemed to draw insects. We kept swatting our arms.
Although the food was extravagantly abundant, very little
of it was being bought. For all the vociferous quarreling
over prices, most of the customers seemed to be haggling
over very small quantities. Only flies and the more
aggressive dogs were feasting.

Conversation was impossible in that pandemonium. I
hoped, in all the commotion, we didn't stand out. We
strolled on, dodging *burros* hitched between stands,
avoiding their plentiful droppings. We bought a string bag

and began filling it with ripe mangoes, slivers of dried fish, some oranges, and a loaf of dark bread.

Finally we found ourselves standing in front of the Café Bayamo, where that clerk's cousin might be a contact for us. The place seemed primarily to be a tavern. It was crowded with military—not at all what we expected. About fifteen soldiers were sitting at tables inside and spilling out onto a patio on the street. When we stepped in, a number of the soldiers turned to look at us. Griffin didn't pause. He walked straight across the large room to the bar and asked the proprietor if we could buy a bottle of water. The proprietor, an elegant old man with several missing teeth, shook his head and said, no, but we could have water for free at a fountain in the park. He added proudly that it was the best water in all of Cuba.

"You didn't ask for Gerardo," I observed as soon as we were outside again.

"You could see the place was crawling with soldiers."

"Why would that clerk send us there?"

"You tell me."

By then it was around noon. We made our way back to the open square in the town center, an expanse of withered yellow grass crisscrossed by gravel paths set among flowery bushes humming with bees. Two barefoot women in black were sitting beside a baby carriage. One of them held a black umbrella open above them. Occasionally the other one leaned forward and fanned the carriage occupant. Some kids were playing soccer. We saw a fountain but it was dry.

There was no shade anywhere. Every tree in sight had been chopped down to an ugly stump. We found seats on a hot wooden bench and stretched our legs out and looked at one another.

"Well?" I said. "Now what?"

"I'm thinking, or trying to."

We dug into the string bag and began eating. Our faces and hands were soon dripping with mango juice.

"Your chest still hurt?" Griffin asked.

"It's okay."

The heat of the sun was intensifying. I was glad we had the fringed *sombreros*. For the most part Bayamo seemed old and worn, rural and languid. From time to time a horse-drawn carriage would pass near the park, hooves clattering on cobblestones or hardened mud. I tried to take it all in. More and more I became absorbed by the plain fact of our finally being in Oriente Province. It gave me a certain odd sense of wonder, mostly because the reason for our entire journey had been raised on a sugar plantation in this province. I pictured him as being an extraordinarily serious student . . .

Griffin interrupted my idle musing by suddenly flinging his orange peels into a bush across the path from us.

"Why are you so remote?" he asked.

"I was just thinking about Fidel."

"Keep your voice down," he whispered, as an old peddler approached with offers of tobacco and lottery coupons.

"Up there somewhere, with his fighters," I finally said. "Anyway, I hope to God they're still up there."

He followed my gaze over the low-lying roofs to the distant blue peaks.

"They have to be. Finding them is our problem," he said. "It's harder than I thought, but we have a few leads."

"What leads?" I wiped my hands on my slacks and dug into my bag for one of my notebooks.

"It's about time you started writing," Griffin said, watching me settle the notebook on my knee and ready a ballpoint. "Just be careful what you write, Paul. You don't know when we might be stopped and your words read."

I nodded absently, considering what he'd just said, wondering what I could possibly write that wouldn't be suspect in the eyes of soldiers or police who might interrogate us. I would have to censor any political observations.

Griffin watched me print "A Novel" on the first page. Stifling an exaggerated yawn, he gave me a hard smack on the thigh and stood up.

"Think I'll roam for awhile," he said. I closed my notebook.

"Alone," he added, "You stay here."

"I'll go with you."

"No. I need to sort some things out, that's all."

"We should stick together." His hand thwarted my rising shoulder.

"Stay here, don't move." he insisted. "I'll be back in an hour."

Before I could protest again he had started rapidly along the path. I slumped back, resigned, uneasy about our being separated. Again I perched the notebook on my knee. At first I had difficulty concentrating, but slowly I drifted into recent memory, squinting down at the white paper, jotting notes recalling specific scenes and moods. A number of pages gradually filled as I sank deeper into a dazed state of reflection that drugged my awareness of the present. I must have lost all sense of time passing. I didn't notice the women with the baby carriage leave, yet they were gone. So were the soccer kids. Certainly an hour must have passed, probably two.

Blinking droplets of sweat from my eyelids, I looked around and tried to estimate just how late it was getting to be. The sun gave no indication. It had bleached the blue sky to a molten white haze. I shaded my eyes against it to see that the nearby stalls were now closed and the streets empty but for a few soldiers standing in strips of shade on the other side of the square. Everything seemed preternaturally quiet, except for some sluggish bumblebees just across the path, droning over the blossoms of a dusty rosebush. Suddenly feeling alarmingly alone and exposed, I put the notebook aside and began flipping bits of gravel at the bees. A tiny hummingbird appeared above the bush, halted in mid-air, a blur of iridescent green suspended over the yellow flowers. It was the first green one I'd ever seen, and evidently I became somewhat hypnotized by its whirring suspension in mid-air because I was exceptionally slow to notice a soldier standing beside me. With grenades affixed to his belt and a rifle suspended from one shoulder, he stood only a few feet from me on the path. It startled me, although he couldn't have been less intimidating. He was just a kid wearing thick-lensed glasses who seemed to be as fascinated as I was by the hummingbird. Smiling amiably, he gestured toward the hummingbird.

"¿Muy cómico, no?"

I smiled back at him and repeated, "Sí, sí, muy cómico."

He chuckled and with a parting nod continued along the path.

My head ached. I threw my arms over the back of the bench, rested my jaw on my chest and soon fell into a sweaty sleep that lasted the remainder of the long afternoon.

It was distinctly cooler when I snapped wide awake with a jolt of alarm. The headache had grown worse. My face was raw and hot, and my stomach queasy. In spite of the discomfort and a certain dizziness, I got to my feet and walked around the perimeter of the park. At nearly every corner there were jeeps that hadn't been there earlier. Heavy machineguns were attached to the hoods, and the vehicles were crammed with soldiers. I had no idea what to do. I strolled past them, not looking at them but peering up each side street that emptied into the square. People were out again. Entering the park was a gaggle of ragged kids lugging shoeshine crates. Nowhere in sight was there anyone resembling Griffin. Sunset looked to be less than an hour away. I was trying not to be frightened. Gradually I returned to the bench and tried to figure whether or not

Bayamo would have a tourist hotel where English might be understood. It didn't seem likely. In any case I needed to stay put and I did, perched indecisively on the edge of the bench, nervously nudging the gravel into little mounds at my feet, trying miserably to contrive a functional plan. It crossed my mind that I might never see Griffin again. The pack of shoeshine boys was coming nearer. In their noisy midst, looking strikingly darker than earlier, was a nonchalant Griffin.

"Get that diary done yet?" he called out.

"Only about six hours ago." I glowered up at him, immense relief quelling the anger.

"Sorry I took so long."

"Where the hell were you?"

He didn't reply. He just winked and sat down beside me. The kids crowded in around us, jabbering and shoving until he had planted each of his feet on a separate shoeshine crate.

"Where the hell were you?" I demanded.

He ignored me, rattling off instructions in Spanish to the two kids squatting at his feet. They began slapping polish onto his boots while the others ran away, shouting frustrated curses.

"They hate your sneakers," he explained. "My god, you are sunburned."

"And you're looking weirdly refreshed," I snarled.

"Oh, that," he agreed, dismissing it. "That's just because I shaved and washed up a bit. Water wasn't hot. For that matter, the meal wasn't anything out of the ordinary either, just a drab sort of commonplace beefsteak with some black beans and cherimoya sherbet. Hardly worth mentioning. Not nearly as exciting as that color you're sporting. Isn't that known as flamingo pink?"

"You're a genuine son of a bitch."

"Now, now," he said, grinning, leaning forward to see how the bootshining was progressing.

115

I flipped open the notebook and pretended to be absorbed in it. This merely amused him even more. Ruffling the hair of one of the boys, he continued a running patter of facetiousness concerning my sunburn and the glorious colors of the island sunsets.

I responded to none of it. With a final flourish of their rags, the shoeshiners stood up and held out blackened palms. Griffin doled out a few coins, then imperiously snapped his fingers. They tore off after the others.

"Listen to me," he said then, tersely. "Don't be pissed off. We're set. Everything's arranged. Everything. We leave in the morning. Our contact says—"

"*What*?" I barked. "Leave for where?"

"That's what I'm telling you. It's all set." He got to his feet. "But right now we better get moving. Come on."

"Wait a minute," I snapped, as he caught my arm, yanking me up off the bench. "What is this contact crap? Where were you all day?"

He tossed my bag at my chest. "We haven't got much time. We're going to eat and sleep in a *posada* tonight. We've got to get there right away, like *now*. Come on."

"Start at the beginning, " I insisted.

"Didn't want to say anything in front of those kids," he said. "There's a curfew about to start. Soldiers have orders to shoot on sight after dark. The last few nights all hell has been breaking loose here. The people have a solid resistance going. They gutted some bar with a bomb last week. Two nights ago they shot a soldier from one of the roofs facing this square. I mean *right here*. Then some lady got her face blown off for whistling out a window for her dog. So just keep walking. I'll fill you in."

"How do you know all this?" I asked.

"We won't be able to talk in the *posada*," he went on almost breathlessly, "so just listen. I spent all afternoon going over it with our contact. She's part of your hero's team. She gave me instructions, very detailed, on how

116

we're to walk into the mountains. Yes, *walk*. It's a risky deal, of course, but she said if we're lucky we'll be with the 26th of July gang in a matter of days."

"How'd you happen to find this so-called 'contact'?"

"Sorry. I have to operate on a need-to-know basis."

"Don't give me that. It's bad enough I had to get sunstroke all day while you fed your face somewhere."

"It really bothers you, huh?" He sounded very pleased. "What a child you are!"

"Keep it up and you'll be sorry, that's how much of a child I am."

"That's the spirit!" He turned an extremely satisfied smile at me as we halted to let a military truck rumble past.

"Now the plan for us getting into the mountains is—"

"Who is this contact?" I interrupted. "I thought we were going to work everything out together."

"We're going into the mountains together," he retorted. "Isn't that enough? Tomorrow morning we leave. Just contemplate that, my surly friend. Tomorrow morning." He gave me a hearty slap on the back as we continued across the street.

"Take it easy," I said. "My back is sautéed."

"You'll be fine, soon as you get some food into you. Sorry you had to wait so long," he said, his voice softening, "but clandestine arrangements take time. You know how it is."

"Do I? I could've gone with you."

"Be realistic," he said. "You don't know Spanish. What could you have done?"

The question was valid but to me beside the point. I tried to see it objectively. We hurried past another gathering of soldiers grouped around the crackling static of a jeep radio, then continued down a side street whose dung-splattered cobblestones wound along between small houses that were scarcely more than hovels. Most of the windows were shuttered. Apparently it was true about the curfew.

"You're angry," Griffin said, breaking several long minutes of bitter silence between us. "Don't let it ruin our last night in civilization. Just trust that I have a solid motive for not telling you too much."

"What does that mean?"

"Isn't it better you don't know about our contact? What if they question you?"

"Why do you think I'd tell them anything you wouldn't?"

"I'm not saying that. Probably you wouldn't. But only one of us has to have the information. Anyway," he rushed on, "It's settled. She said everything would be arranged. She's done this before for journalists. They're very interested in journalists. It's perfect, Paul. You should be thanking me. We're right where we want to be."

* * *

The orders from our contact, called *La Negrita* by Griffin, were for us to leave Bayamo at exactly nine o'clock in the morning. After fidgeting over *pan dulce* and *café con leche* at the *posada,* we found our way to the post office and mailed letters to our families. Then we strolled through the shabby outskirts of town and proceeded on into the open countryside. I left most of my books in the hotel, to lighten my bag. Our destination was supposed to be a tiny village located at the base of the foothills some fifteen kilometers away, in the direction of the visible Pico Turquino, highest peak in the Sierra Maestra range.

La Negrita had warned Griffin there were often surprise movements of army units throughout the foothills. We were to stay on full alert for them and for helicopters, but it was impossible to imagine any danger beyond lizard bites in that flat, almost treeless farmland. The dew had already burned off the recently plowed fields on either side of the dirt road. The soil was a rich, moist loam, almost black. It appeared to be wonderfully fertile. The entire terrain around us was profoundly peaceful beneath a cloudless azure sky. Insects whirring and the occasional cries of songbirds added to the hushed air of languor spread over our route. The road itself was little more than two baked mud tire ruts threading the fields. Directly ahead of us and sweeping around to our right were the foothills, rolling up toward the long series of pale violet crags behind them. Ahead of us several hawks were gliding in lazy majestic circles. We hiked along feeling unusually comfortable together, one of us occasionally whistling or swatting at the white butterflies that seemed to be vying with the occasional hovering dragonfly. Little lizards sunned themselves in hoofprints marking the hardened road. "Who owns all this land?" Griffin asked. "You have any idea?"

"Rich foreigners probably," I said. "That's what I've read. Nearly half of Cuban farmland is owned by foreigners. The rest by wealthy locals."

"*Latifundismo*," he said. "All the actual farmer workers are peasants who don't own anything."

"In this interview I read," I said, "Castro described Cuba as a single crop economy with a single trade partner, an economic disaster. He wants to change all that."

Just ahead of us, an unidentifiable green snake went slithering across the path into the slack reeds growing from shallow ditches bordering the road.

"You know," Griffin said lazily, "they were my favorite animal when I was a kid. Snakes. Not necessarily poisonous ones. I just liked them. What was yours?"

"Oh, panthers, I guess, or jaguars. I saw them in the Pittsburgh zoo. Their grace and power seemed to me pretty terrific—it was everything I wasn't. I saw myself as too tall and not well coordinated."

"I identified with snakes," Griffin said. "Silent, lowdown. Everyone hates them, but I never thought they were especially evil. What if a snake did tempt Eve? All the more reason to admire them."

"Did your folks go to church? Isn't Puerto Rico a Catholic country?"

"It's not really a country. They call it a territory. As if every country and every island on earth isn't a territory. Anyway, my mother was Catholic, my father an atheist. After awhile he refused to go with her to church, so she stopped going, but we always prayed before meals and she had me praying at night when I got into bed. I stopped all the Hail Marys when my brother died."

"By the way," I interrupted him, "Shouldn't we be seeing that bottling factory by now?"

We were watching for a Hatuey Beer plant. Just before it there was supposed to be a road branching off to the right, leading directly into a village in the foothills. That was our destination.

"You lost your faith?" I asked.

"Never had any," he replied, "but I was willing to go through the rituals for my mother. They seemed harmless. She liked me doing it."

"When did you start considering yourself sort of an outsider?"

"It came naturally, just growing up, being observant. The hypocrisy everywhere, the self-satisfaction, that North American presumption of superiority. Not to mention the racism. In Puerto Rico I wondered about all the poor people. Before they got me into this special school for the brats of US military and diplomats, before that I went to a regular public school."

"You're sure about this contact?"

"Very sure," he said. "She was impressive. Don't worry, you're just being impatient."

He reached down and picked a couple of long blades of grass from the side of the road. After fitting one between his teeth, he handed the other to me. It had a bitter taste.

"Tell me something, Paul."

"Yeah?"

"What did you write to your folks?"

"Nothing much, just letting them know I'm still alive. I didn't want to say too much. My mother will be glad to hear from me. She'll be completely mystified by the postmark. My father will just be mildly relieved he won't be seeing me in the mill again any time soon."

"Well," Griffin said, "with my father, I laid it right on the line before we left. Clear and simple."

"What on earth did you say to him?"

"Just setting matters straight. What the hell, at the very least he's paying the taxes that buy dictators' weapons and train soldiers for the empire. Even worse, he has some kind of high security government job. That puts him on the side of the enemy. For years now I've resisted his bullshit, his wanting to appear to have humanitarian principles without ever backing them up. That's all over."

I thought about that, still chewing on the blade of grass.

"For me I think it was in the first year of high school," I said, "I was bothered by one of my teachers referring to democracy and capitalism as the fundamental standards of America. I didn't get it. Even by that teacher's definitions, they seemed to oppose one another. How can you have democracy with such huge differences in income, in personal wealth? I argued about it, but that teacher didn't want to hear it."

"Back then," Griffin said, "did you ever think sometime you'd be doing something like this?"

"You asked me that last night."

"I forget what you said."

"I said I'd never even dreamed of anything like this. Never. I thought about foreign places, of course. They interested me, but Anna wasn't enthusiastic. Her childhood in Europe after the war only made her appreciate Pittsburgh all the more. Then too, she wanted children.

Mostly I just wanted to be a good man, a good worker, a good husband and the best-hitting third baseman in Pennsylvania."

"Not me," Griffin said. "Even in grade school I was certain I'd do great things. I've always known it. Whether it's dance or drama, you know I have to be excelling at something."

"I don't doubt it."

"And here we are," he said, punching me lightly on the arm. "I'm glad you talked me into this."

"Me too."

"Sometimes I think about our first meeting," he said after a moment. "Odd how it's all worked out."

I nodded somewhat inattentively. I was trying to make out what the structure ahead of us was.

Through shimmering heat waves there slowly emerged the shape of a large building. As we drew closer I could see the Cerveza Hatuey sign on top of it, but no indication of another road. Then I noticed the tank parked in the shade on the side of the building. Its massive treads weren't moving. Its long cannon pointed at the mountains.

I yanked Griffin's arm, sending us both stumbling into the ditch, into a shallow trickle of brown water that stank and soaked our shoes and stained our pants.

"Think they saw us?" he said.

"No idea."

"Well, you're the ROTC ace. What do you do about tanks?"

"Stay out of their way."

"How do we do that?"

"Just stay down."

He turned and peeked out through parted reeds. "It's there, all right. *Big* goddam mother. Bunch of soldiers sitting around, playing cards or something."

"Is there a road?" I asked, edging up beside him to see for myself. There were at least ten soldiers lounging in the shade of the building. One of them was basking in the open hatch on top of the tank, smoking a cigarette. Apparently no one had seen us.

"There's a road," I said after a moment. "La Negrita was right about that, but they've got it blocked off. We'll have to get across this field and find the road further along."

"Couldn't Castro use that big mama?" he said.

"Can you shut up and think for a minute?" I said.

"We'll have to keep to this ditch," he pointed out, "but it's full of fertilizer. We can't hide until nightfall. They're not paying attention, we can make a run for it. There's no other way."

"Tanks have machine guns, moron."

"Let them try," he snorted, jumping into open view, his bag tucked under his arm.

"Come on!" He took off running full speed across the furrows, heading for a far horizon of low trees at the edge of the foothills. Then I too was out of the ditch and sprinting recklessly after him, clutching my bag, running as fast as I could. He had a considerable lead but he was swerving as if dodging bullets, while I ran in a straight line. With each breath I expected to hear the tank's engine start up, or for a shell to be lobbed in our direction, yet I didn't look back. The furrows would trip me if my boots didn't hit the tops of them just right. Griffin galloped over two with every stride, although his boots were carrying a weight of mud, slowing his momentum, as did the fancy zigzagging. I was narrowing his lead. I remembered racing with him back at college. As quickly as this thought occurred, it was forgotten when I heard shouting and rifle shots. Spurred to even more frantic speed, I vaulted over some irrigation pipes and glanced up to see Griffin only a few yards ahead.

Beyond him, much closer now, loomed the mountains. I caught my second wind and sprinted up alongside him. More shots rang out. Griffin stopped swerving and ran straight beside me. We were gasping for breath but somehow managed to stay upright across the final stretch in the open before we plunged into a grove of green banana trees and finally pitched to the ground in coarse long grass. There we sprawled, breathing hard, until I forced myself up to see if the tank had moved, or if any of the soldiers were coming after us. I couldn't tell. They were no longer in sight, and the only sound was our hoarse panting. I collapsed back onto the grass.

"I don't think they're following us."

"Damn boots," Griffin wheezed.

I opened my eyes and rolled over to see dark green fronds patterned against blue sky overhead. From the nearest tree I yanked off a bunch of four little green bananas and peeled one. Still hard, no discernible flavor. I handed the rest of them to Griffin.

"*Plátanos,*" he said. "*Gracias.* Now to find our road." He coughed and rolled over and heaved himself onto his feet.

After a bit of looking we came upon the road, again little more than two parallel tire paths through the grass. It led us out of the grove and into a stretch of wild trees and thorny bushes, and it wasn't long before we became aware of a peculiar thing. Before that mad dash, nearly everything had appeared to be some shade of brown or yellow, while the foothills had looked as though they rose just beyond the fields, but this new track toward them was gradually dipping downward, taking us into an inexplicably swampy region. Tropical plants and trees began appearing in increasingly dense profusion on both sides of those tire tracks. After two or three kilometers of steady, slow descent, the air itself seemed to be degenerating into ever steamier humidity. We were now sweating heavily and swatting at bugs. Doubts about the directions kept occuring, but I kept quiet, hoping we'd soon start climbing. Instead we kept going downward until we were deep into something like a swamp. Still we sloshed on, mopping sweat from our faces and squinting anxiously ahead until encroaching vines and other foliage slowed us down considerably. Except for sticky red flowers growing on thorny vines, everything around us was some shade of green. The muck grabbed our feet and threatened to swallow our shoes.

"This contact of yours," I said at last, "she happen to mention anything about a jungle."

"You worried?" he said over his shoulder.

"Just wondering."

"Well, stop worrying."

"What about crocodiles?" I said, "or alligators?"

"Haven't seen any."

All around us water dripped and gurgled, while overhead the patches of sky began diminishing, everything somewhat darkening. I was nearly convinced that either we had deviated from our instructions or been deliberately sent into some gruesome dead end when Griffin finally stopped to light a cigarillo. He eyed me over the flame of a wooden match.

"Well," he said, "what do you think? Have we gone seven kilometers?"

"You tell me, Bwana. You're the one who spent all day yesterday arranging this jaunt."

"That's about four miles," he said. "I don't think we've gone that far."

He dropped the match into a puddle, wiped the sweat from his forehead with his shirt-tail, took a deep drag and exhaled, sending smoke into the vegetation.

"I think you've blundered us into some rainforest," I said. "Did you even ask about our need for food?"

"Think we could have passed the first hut somehow without seeing it?"

"There are no huts," I snorted. "I mean, given your vaunted infallibility, is it even remotely possible you made a little mistake in understanding the directions?"

"Not possible."

"Your contact couldn't have been some impostor?"

"Not possible," he replied, drawing again on the cigarillo.

"You're certain?"

"Positive."

"In that case," I said, "we keep slogging, but it's certainly odd she didn't mention any stretch of swamp." I moved irritably around him and he started after me, descending still deeper into this quagmire. I was determined to hear him acknowledge some error.

"If you get tired of martyrdom," he said at one point, "maybe we can discuss this."

"You admit we're lost?" I said. "In tropical slop? Because you fucked up?"

There was no answer. Suddenly I felt sorry for him, and more than a little worried. Both of us were badly in need of rest, yet we sloshed on, clothes sopping, leg muscles numb with what had become almost wading. Finally we became aware that we were moving almost imperceptibly upward. The air was becoming less moist and sticky, the foliage less dense. In the backs of my knees I could feel an added strain indicating we were beginning to climb. Another quarter of an hour or so and the track began to dry out and widen again.

Not long after that we reached a small clearing from which we could see for a considerable distance. We were in the lower foothills. We paused, deeply relieved to note the sky still held ample daylight. Not much later we finally reached the promised shack. It had a thick thatched roof and sat alone in a small clearing.

"Don't pretend you don't see it," Griffin shouted jubilantly from behind me. "Take a long, contrite look at it, oh you doubting Bell. That is a *bohio*, my friend, an abandoned one, as promised. It means we're almost to the village. Once again, I am proven right."

"Are you kidding?" I scoffed. "You were wondering too. Just admit it."

"Nope," he chortled, "I entirely trusted the splendid La Negrita. Oh ye of little faith. But I do understand how depressing it must be for you, my being right all the time. Perfection in a friend is hard to bear."

"I can live with it," I said, still immensely relieved to have found the shack.

Reinvigorated, I followed him up one steep slope after another, until the path broadened into more of an unpaved road and we began passing more huts. All the *bohios* were primitive. Beneath thatched roofs they were constructed of dried strips of palm fronds woven around wooden poles sunk in the ground. Each was somewhat secluded in its own small clearing among dense clusters of dwarf palmettos. Between them were garden plots. From one hut came sounds of a quarrel. From another, sounds of a radio broadcasting a rumba through a lot of static. A couple of the clearings were strewn with articles of clothing spread over tufts of lank grass to dry in the sunlight. Chickens strutted around them. A saddled *burro* lazily rubbed its rump against a tree trunk. In a mudhole near the last *bohio* several piglets nuzzled at the belly of an outstretched sow. The sixth *bohio* on the right.

"You're sure this is it?" I said. No one seemed to be home. In the shade of the hut's open doorway a pregnant dog lay panting, flicking her tail at flies. Griffin shouted out *hola* and the dog growled. A moment later a middle-aged man appeared in the doorway, a muscular, lightskinned Negro with red-rimmed eyes.

"*Buenos días, señor,*" Griffin said to him.

"*Buenas,*" the man drawled in reply, crouching on his heels to pet the dog.

"*¿Tiene usted un poco de agua?*" asked Griffin.

The man busied himself stroking the dog's enlarged belly, but she refused to be soothed. With a gutteral growl, she rolled onto her feet and slowly backed away from us, showing teeth below a curled upper lip.

"*Señor,*" Griffin repeated uneasily, "*¿Por favor, tiene usted agua?*"

Slowly the man straightened up and looked us over. Griffin handed him a piece of paper he'd been given by our contact. With a mere glance at the signature on it, the man stepped back with no change of expression and motioned us into the hut. Inside was a single room with a plastic shower curtain separating part of it. The man went behind it, and we could hear him speaking quietly to someone. The interior was dank and cool and clean—as clean at least as dirt can be. A very old woman was raking the earthen floor with a rustic broom. She nodded gravely. There was only one orthodox piece of furniture, a double bed with a lumpy straw mattress. A packing crate was being used as a table, two wooden packing crates as chairs. A rusted gallon can held a single bird of paradise blossom. On one wall was a framed picture of a pink-cheeked Jesus standing on a cumulus cloud. The quiet discussion ceased as a middle-aged woman with a faint mustache stepped from behind the shower curtain and smiled at us.

"*Señores, bienvenidos,*" she said. "*¿Ustedes quieren agua?*"

I nodded eagerly.

"*Por favor, señora,*" Griffin said.

She handed him a long metal dipper and motioned to a large clay jug. Then she excused herself and left. We seated ourselves on the wooden boxes. The water tasted slightly of iron but was cold and delicious and we didn't stop taking turns emptying the dipper until the woman with the mustache returned with two bowls full of something like mashed potatoes. A dark-skinned boy about my age came in. He introduced himself as José. We stood up to shake hands but he ignored the gesture and began rattling Spanish at Griffin in a staccato tone of authority. He was wearing a dirty white shirt and Levis, with a ragged straw *sombrero* like ours. A machete was wedged under his belt. He was all business.

"We leave in a few minutes," Griffin informed me. "He's going to guide us into the mountains. Don't make faces. The woman is his mother. He's angry because we're so late. It seems we were expected two hours ago. He says now we'll have to hike after dark. How we could've gotten here any earlier I don't know, but don't argue. José doesn't much like Yankees. Finish that *malanga* now. I have a hunch we'll need the energy."

"This is *malanga*?"

"Yeah, *malanga* root, without salt," he said. "It's a tuber. They eat a lot of it in the Caribbean. They had it in Puerto Rico. Poor people ate it, but with salt."

Behind the shower curtain a passage led into a kitchen shed extending from the rear of the shack. Woodsmoke from an open firepit obscured things but we could still see the older man, possibly José's father, stretched out snoring on a mat surrounded by chickens. We set about repacking some of the things in our bags.

"You might want to scrap those notebooks," Griffin advised. "We have to travel ultra-light."

I had no intention of getting rid of them, yet we left behind nearly everything else we'd salvaged from customs, keeping barely a change of clothes. Neither of us had spare shoes. I'd lost my sunglasses. Griffin had lost his camera. With the bags slung over our shoulders once again, we brushed the plastic curtain aside and stepped back into the main part of the hut where José was waiting. We handed his mother the empty bowls and thanked her. José bent over to kiss her forehead. For a moment her eyes closed tight. Then she opened them and looking directly at me, she asked me something in Spanish.

"How old are you?" Griffin translated. "Where is your mother?"

129

While José pointedly scuffed his feet in the doorway, I muttered something a bit garbled. As Griffin translated my reply, the woman nodded solemnly and said something else.

"She's going to pray the Virgin will let your mother see you again," Griffin said. "*Temprano,* she says, meaning *soon,* because you look so young and innocent. Don't just stand there. Hug her or something. Let's get this show on the road."

"*Gracias, señora,*" I said. "*Muchas gracias.*" I caught her hand and kissed the back of it. She laughed.

"*Adios, señora,*" Griffin added, neatly tipping his *sombrero* while giving me a good nudge toward the door.

Already the remaining daylight was vanishing into long, damp blue shadows. I was startled to find nearly fifteen people standing around outside, looking at us, waving to us.

"*Buena suerte, periodistas,*" called several of them.

"*¡Que les vaya bien!*" called others.

We waved back and thanked them, while flocks of little birds were filling the trees with evening cries. José was moving forward without a single glance back to ensure we were keeping up. We were, but barely, and only with increasing difficulty as the sun vanished, replaced eventually by millions of stars. José was a skilled hiker who seemed to know the way well, and he wasn't interested in showing us mercy, although a few times he stopped and waited, or paused to warn us about specific difficulties ahead. For the most part, there was no path, no trail. We were moving over fairly even ground, which gave way to several stretches of climbing steep hillsides or scrambling across rock faces or walking through groves of trees whose thick roots spread out above the ground. They tripped us several times. Fortunately, the ground was mostly dry. Once in the dark we skirted a village entirely without lights. No fires were visible, although we could smell woodsmoke.

I had the feeling there were other settlements nearby, and many other shacks along the way, possibly even roads. Mystifyingly, José had us avoiding them.

At one point while we were finding our way over the mossy stones of a nearly dry creek bed, Griffin sprained his right ankle. He shouted an impulsive curse that brought José rushing back to warn us to be quiet. Griffin murmured something to José indicating he understood, but he didn't acknowledge the sprain. We carried on climbing, nearly always climbing. When finally we dropped down to rest, we found ourselves on a stony plateau overlooking a valley largely concealed by mist. There were clouds below us, yet above us the stars were out in abundance, along with three-quarters of the moon. While it felt as though we might have reached a considerable altitude, this wasn't at all certain. We couldn't see anything in the valley below. There was a warm breeze just strong enough to keep mosquitos away.

José immediately curled up and, using one arm as a pillow, appeared to fall asleep at once. We were exhausted but keyed up. Griffin admitted his ankle was throbbing. One of my trouser legs was torn, dangling from the knee down. Along my calf was a shallow gash, probably from a branch or thorn, leaving blood seeping down into one shoe. Through a fissure in the rock face near us water was sluicing down. I sloshed handfuls of it over my leg. The cold offset some of the pain, then I washed my face and arms with the scrap torn off my trousers, dipping it in the swift water. I took off my shoes with difficulty, peeled down the socks and delicately pulled them off to find each foot was an ugly mass of watery red blisters surrounded by dirt and loose rolls of skin.

When I'd finished washing I took the cloth, sopping wet, back to Griffin, only to find him sound asleep. Some of the doubts I'd been having appeared again. I had hiked through woods—even dense woods like these—many times, but always over relatively known terrain, and when necessary I'd had a map, a compass and a sheath knife, often a flashlight, matches, a canteen, and water purification pills. I wondered why Griffin agreed to this way of proceeding and why I went along with it. It seemed unnecessarily reckless. I guess I assumed we'd find help once we got into the mountains. Did La Negrita understand that we weren't equipped for hiking like this? Feeling stupid and angry, mostly at myself, I soon drifted into a dreamless sleep.

We were awakened at dawn by the distant cries of a rooster rising from the valley below. José was standing over Griffin, prodding him in the ribs with the toe of his shoe, saying, *"Arriba, hombre, arriba ahora."*

Griffin stared up at him through a bloodshot eye and groaned.

"¡Rápido!" José prodded. *"¡Vámonos, muchachos!"*

Moaning, Griffin sat up and began exploring with his fingers the cut and swollen places on his head. He seemed to be in worse shape than I was. Several minutes passed before he looked around at me, at José, and then at the sky.

"Bullshit," he said.

"That's the spirit," I said.

"Bullshit!" he said again.

"Arriba, hombre," José kept goading, until Griffin lashed back at him in a savage Spanish I couldn't begin to understand. This erupted into a quarrel that only ended when José turned away and started back into the woods above us.

"What was that about?" I asked.

"He wants to go all the rest of the way up to La Plata without another stop. And by the way, he volunteered the information that the La Plata we're going to isn't the same as the larger town near the coast. He said we should know this in case we get lost."

"Did you let him know about your ankle?"

"Nope."

"Then I'm going to tell him. How do you say 'ankle' in Spanish?"

He hoisted my *sombrero*, hanging on my back by a string around my neck, and clamped it down hard onto my head. "Keep that on," he ordered. You're already burned."

"Tell me the word."

"Forget it," he said. "Let's go, before he leaves us alone here."

"Think he's actually with the 26th of July Movement?"

He ignored the question, getting to his feet grimacing with pain and stoic resolution.

"¡Más rápido!" called José, already well ahead of us. *"¡Vámonos, muchachos!"*

"One *momentito*, shithead," yelled Griffin.

José never permitted either of us to quite catch up to him. It was humiliating. I thought he might simply abandon us. This spurred us to keep up. If one or the other of us managed to get close, José would increase his pace until we were forced to fall behind again. This obsessive progress of his was infuriating, even if it did have the effect of getting us to cover a lot of ground. Still, his attitude implanted a steadily deepening anger that seemed pointless and thoroughly destructive. We barely talked, not even to complain. Our only nourishment was wild green oranges with inch-thick skins and juice too sour to swallow without wincing. Now and then we ate a sort of dwarf banana as we hurried on. Luckily, we came upon numerous creeks whose water seemed fresh.

Only once before midday did we pause. We'd been plodding up a ridge clotted with tall shrubs and trees whose spreading roots slowed us, when over the sound of our labored breathing we heard voices. Three men suddenly appeared directly above us, climbing down rapidly. José didn't try to take cover. We stopped to watch them descend. They greeted our guide with an excited flurry of handshaking and breathless talk. They were rebels, wearing stained khaki shirts and black berets. Two of them had rifles slung over their shoulders, plus black and red armbands with *"26 de Julio"* boldly painted on them in white. The oldest one, probably thirty years old, was armed with a decrepit-looking revolver strapped into a crude holster. Wiry and athletic, they all had the mixed blood coloration I was seeing in most Cubans, along with facial stubble, not yet beards. The wind had them holding their black berets clamped onto their heads.

"*Hola,*" one of them shouted down to us as they left José and came down the ridge toward us.

"*Hola, hola, amigos. Bienvenidos.*"

Even before José introduced us, the rebels surrounded us, cheerfully slapping our backs and bewildering us with questions as they grabbed eagerly for our hands, greeting us like the warmest of old friends. They seemed to have no reservations whatsoever about our being *norteamericanos*. They were enthusiastically welcoming. I'd never felt such immediate warmth from total strangers.

"What's he saying?" I urged Griffin. "Tell me."

Griffin frowned at me. "I'll tell you later."

One of them took from his shirt pocket a morsel of dark chocolate coated with lint and tobacco shreds. He broke it in half, brushed half of it on his shirtsleeve, and offered it to me. I broke it again into two pieces and gave Griffin one of them. He was rattling off answers to the questions of the older one, so I just stood there not understanding the conversation but not much bothered about it.

Then José shouted something.

"*Luego, hermanos,*" one of the rebels said.

"*Venceremos, patria o muerte,*" shouted another, and they trotted on down along the ridge. José resumed climbing, the two of us at his heels.

"Brothers," Griffin then explained. "They called us brothers. They think Fidel is at La Plata, maybe eight hours from here."

"Eight hours hiking," I said.

"I'm guessing that's what they meant. They also told me José has us hiking in daylight because we don't know these mountains. They usually travel by night. It's a lot safer. Planes can't see you, but José doesn't want to see us with a broken leg or fractured skull."

"Very cool guys," I said. "They didn't even check our IDs."

"They knew about us. Someone must have telephoned or something."

From that ridge we climbed down into a sun-splashed valley where corn was growing in long rows. Vast acres of tobacco looked ready for harvesting. We heard what was probably a tractor but never saw it. José pushed us hard over that flat ground until we finally paused near a small pond where two white Tuscan-type bulls, the kind with humps, were tethered to an empty cart. José produced a tin cup and assured Griffin the pond water was good to drink.

It was already dark by the time we reached the end of that valley and came upon what Griffin called *una finca,* a sort of primitive plantation comprised of several barns, a few *bohios*, a pen with several hogs, and a pasture where cows and a few donkeys were grazing. Approaching the largest shack, we crossed a flat area paved with concrete and covered by coffee beans, both red and green, either drying or ripening in the sun. A man raking them, a real mountain *guajiro*, stopped when he saw us and hurried into the house. A few minutes later a woman came out and hugged José before welcoming us. She was middle-aged, dark, and cheerful. We followed her into the house and sat down on wooden chairs with woven straw seats at a large wooden table. Griffin had a conversation with her before she excused herself and left the room. Soon there was the potent rich smell of very strong coffee. She passed around a tray with tiny cups and a pot with a wooden handle.

Sipping that sweet thick coffee, I looked at Griffin. He was gingerly massaging his bad ankle.

"Is it any better?" I asked him.

"Couldn't be better," he said. "We'll be sleeping in the barn tonight. They even have blankets for us, although we have to leave early. First light."

"Good news," I said, "but you didn't answer my question."

"We're going to be eating soon," he said. "Think you can handle some *bacalao Cubano*?"

"If it's food, I can handle it."

"It's the best food in the world," he replied. "Rice with beans and tomatoes and lemons and onions and garlic and salted codfish. And probably more coffee."

"How does one say in Spanish—'I am insanely happy to hear this'?"

A dawn cloudburst delayed our departure. It broke torrentially, turning the sky dark, pounding hard on the barn roof, frightening the animals. It created huge puddles and patches of mud before the sun came out, creating a steaminess throughout the valley, and perilous going on our trail. José was determined to push us, but either he was giving us a break or our lungs were becoming conditioned, because we were now managing to keep up with him with less difficulty. Griffin's ankle had been properly bandaged by the woman who'd served us food. She'd even found a spare pair of thick cotton socks and some ointment. We moved in a single file, climbing steadily upward, resting only a few minutes every hour or so.

José remained insistent about our not talking, so I concentrated on the terrain, all the time wishing I'd brought a guidebook that might identify all the trees and plants I'd never before seen. Easily the most distinctive was a tree with an astonishing sprawl of roots above ground level, a thorny trunk and giant pods, some of which were open, revealing hefty tufts of white cottony substance. When we paused near one of them to catch our breath, I noticed that José spread his arms against the tree and kissed the bark. I asked Griffin to ask him why he did that. José replied that the tree was a sacred *árbol de ceiba*. I got a noisy snort of ridicule out of Griffin when I planted, impulsively, my own kiss on that colossal tree.

The sky was intensely blue. There was ample wind keeping the clouds scooting right along, constantly changing shape, but I couldn't keep an eye on their formations without my shoes getting promptly clogged with mud.

8

Early April, 1958

Subdued voices, the distinct smell of meat sizzling in old lard, the shadowy orange glow of a kerosene lantern—these were the first things I noticed on waking. I was stretched out on a prickly straw mattress laid on damp earth inside a *bohio,* a pair of bare brown feet near my head, very large feet. The big toe of one was scratching the heel of the other. Stiffly I rolled over and propped myself on one elbow to find several dark, grizzled men sitting on chairs around a large wooden table. These were *guajiros,* mountain people, prematurely weathered and oddly impassive. They watched me as I rubbed my eyes, trying to get oriented. We'd hiked until almost dark to get to this settlement fairly high in the mountains. I dimly remembered lying down to rest.

"You're finally awake," said Griffin, edging into view. A little boy maybe ten or eleven years old was holding his hand.

"Come on," he said to me. "*Arriba* and shine. Meet my buddy here, our new guide, Lobito."

The boy was even darker than the men around him. He had bright white teeth, nearly black eyes, and a burnt caramel skin tone very like Griffin's. I got to my feet and reached out a hand to the boy. He grasped it immediately, shook it formally twice up and down and grinned.

Griffin said. "You better get washed up. We'll be eating soon." Lobito grabbed Griffin's hand again.

"Our new guide?" I asked. "What happened to José?"

"He had to get back. He said he'd see us later. He wished us good luck."

I shook hands with each of the men. One by one they told me their names. I hoped my nap hadn't held up their supper. Then Griffin, Lobito, and I stepped out the open doorway into the shadows of late dusk. Griffin got a cigarillo going and stood smoking in silence. The dirt road curved between several other shacks, all thatched except for one with a corrugated tin roof. Through their walls leaked a thousand tiny specks of lantern light, the purple shapes of the hills looming around us.

Lobito led us down a grassy embankment to the edge of a sandy stream whose surface was calm enough to reflect the evening sky. I squatted while I washed, surprised at all the scratches and bite marks on my arms and legs, some of which looked infected.

"It's annoying," Griffin said from behind me. "They told me there are settlements and tiny villages like this one scattered all through the mountains. We could have stopped at any of them and gotten all the food and rest we needed. The *guajiros* would have been happy to see us. That's what they said. But no, José had to cripple us."

"How's that ankle? That was a nasty sprain."

"When I first woke up it was too swollen to get a boot onto my foot. Lobito helped me bandage it. These *guajiros* couldn't believe José treated us like that. They think it will be much easier for us with Lobito."

"Isn't he sort of young to be a guide?" I said.

"He's thirteen, and very proud to be part of the movement. It means everything to him."

"Where are his parents? " I asked.

"He's an orphan," Griffin said quietly. "*Un huérfano.* About a year ago his entire family was killed, not that far from here. Planes fly over this valley every couple of days and sometimes they drop bombs on anything that looks alive—people, cows, anything. You can imagine what napalm does to thatched huts."

"I can imagine," I said, but I really couldn't. I'd never heard of napalm.

"It's a kind of explosive jelly," Griffin explained. "Our little pal was on his way back from school, some little school the rebels started for the kids around here, when he heard a plane. There was an explosion somewhere near him, they told me, and he lit out for home. When he got within sight of his family's *bohio* there was fire spreading over the whole hillside. His family tried to get out—his parents and a grandmother—but the fire spread too fast. Fidel's group took him in. They've been his family ever since. In some ways he's older than we are. I really like the little guy."

"He knows these mountains?"

"I asked the same question. They said Lobito knows only two routes, two that so far are safe. You never know when an army unit might appear, but they haven't been seen on these routes, and Lobito is very careful. One goes from here up to La Plata, where Fidel's troop has a sort of base. I don't know about the other one. They said he's terrifically proud to be doing this. His name means 'little wolf,' by the way. The rebels gave him that name. They said he was in shock at first, mute, never responding. Weeks went by. You can see how much that's changed. He's still quiet though."

I straightened up wondering how I was going to dry myself. The stream had a slightly polluted smell. I shook my head briskly and flung my arms around.

"They gave me a towel," Griffin said. "You can use that. Anyway, not a single one of his family made it. And this little guy saw it all."

I didn't know what to say. The story sounded true enough, and something in the boy's eyes verified it. I knew what it was to lose one person you loved, but this was too grotesque to be real to me. We started back up the embankment toward the shacks. Griffin led the way, Lobito holding his hand.

In the *bohio* at least eight men were now seated around a table loaded with steaming platters of food. Two chairs were empty. The air was a dense haze of smoke and the mellow conversation of men long accustomed to being together. Several children had come in and were gaping at us. Four older women in black dresses veered around them, scuttling back and forth from the open fires to the table with yet more food. One of the men rose solemnly to his feet and looked around, nodding, then motioned for us to be seated. The others fell silent, expectant. The women ceased moving. We took the two places of honor facing each other from opposite ends of the table. Once settled, Griffin hauled Lobito onto his lap and I lifted the crude wooden spoon in front of me, then hesitated, wondering if they said grace.

Our host stammered out a few sentences of welcome. As soon as he'd finished, Griffin graciously thanked him and said in Spanish, as he later explained, that we were very eager to share the food of the *guajiros* because we hoped to gain from it some of their well-known strength and great courage. Sounds of approval filled the room. Nearly all of them wore little gold crucifixes or saints' medallions on soiled strings around their throats or pinned to their shirts.

"*Caballeros*," the host said, setting before us small bowls of steaming *malanga* covered with bits of wild rabbit and shards of steamed greenery. Then the others were served.

"*Caballeros, niños, silencio por favor*," resumed the host. The women hushed the children. Giggling and whining ceased. Everything grew very quiet. Our host solemnly lowered his head and put his hands together as if he was about to say grace.

"*Viva la Revolución*," he said gravely. "*Viva Fidel Castro*."

A swift chatter of assent broke from the others. The man on my left struck his wooden spoon sharply against mine.

"*De acuerdo,*" he said. "*Viva también los periodistas norteamericanos. ¡Viva!*"

Nearly all the men nodded enthusiastically. Calloused and crusty hands began thrusting in front of us heaping plates of yucca and fried slices of *plátano*, followed by bowls of a garlicky bean stew laced with burned rice. For a long moment in the midst of eating, over the smoking spread of mountain food and outstretched arms, Griffin and I paused to look at one another. His eyes were shining. Probably mine were too. Lobito was holding a spoon filled with stew up to Griffin's mouth.

* * *

It was so near dawn that the sun had not yet burned off the last cool traces of morning mist. Birds in nearby fruit trees were singing energetically. Most of the men were already at work in the higher up mango and banana groves, or inspecting beehives, or picking up new supplies of coffee and tobacco. Only one, a blind grandfather, remained behind. The village women were taking armloads of laundry down to the stream. Their number surprised us. We'd seen only five or six women the night before, while now there were at least fifteen and perhaps twenty girls and women kneeling over the water, pounding sodden clothes against stones, then rinsing them and pounding again. From the doorway, sipping thick coffee from small glasses, we could see them talking animatedly among themselves, pointedly ignoring us. Every now and then, one of the younger women threw a furtive glance in our direction. Griffin made a big production of tipping his *sombrero* and smiling. Each time a chorus of teasing and scolding from the older women compelled the girl to resume working.

"They're like the *campesinas* in Puerto Rico," Griffin remarked. "For a few years, around fifteen to eighteen, you can't be within sight of them without desiring them. Like that one on the end there in the pink blouse, the one that was just giving me the eye. They're ripe and juicy. They can turn you into a sex maniac just by pouting. But after that single lush period, they tend to wither. Tapeworms and babies and—you ready? Looks like he's got our animals ready to go."

I nodded and set my glass on the ground just inside the shack. Lobito had finished rigging three donkeys and was approaching us, leading them. He'd insisted on handling the whole chore by himself. Not that Griffin or I would have been much help. Neither of us had ever ridden a donkey, or a horse. When we tried the previous evening to explain this to the incredulous *guajiros*, they assumed we were joking. In a country as rich as America, one of them said, surely everyone had many horses and donkeys, which they called *burros*. They insisted on loaning us their animals so Griffin's ankle would have more chance to heal before we reached La Plata.

Lobito ducked silently past us into the hut, and returned with a chair and two sets of steel spurs. His tongue was set at the corner of his lips as he handed each of us a pair of spurs and pointed at the ones he was wearing, presumably demonstrating how they were to be put on. We gave them a try. Mine wouldn't clamp on over my shoes and Griffin's swollen foot wouldn't hold one. Hence we were wearing only one spur between us when we walked over to the two donkeys, both chestnut-colored, with straw mats folded in place of saddles. Lobito's mount was dark gray and much smaller. He followed with the chair and waited with a delighted grin as we warily patted the bony foreheads of the two larger animals.

"Ask him," I said, "if they buck."

"You ask him."

He turned to praise the boy's work. "*Está bien, chico,*" he said warmly, "*muy, muy bien.*"

The boy set the chair down and stepped onto it, then smoothly swung onto his donkey's back, hesitated, then offered a dutiful wave of his white *sombrero* to the women watching us from the stream.

"*Vaya con Dios, niño,*" they cried. "*Buena suerte.*"

The boy donned his *sombrero*, made a clucking noise, and bounced his spurs off the *burro's* ribs. It began ambling forward along the road. Our *burros* followed, before we had a chance to mount them.

"*Hasta la vista, señores,*" the women shouted. The younger ones waved bits of laundry.

"*Buen viaje. Vaya con Dios.*"

"*Muchas gracias,*" we called back, clumsily getting ourselves seated on the animals.

Lobito moved at a brisker gait as we rode out of the settlement, out *burros* now holding to that pace as they followed the road higher into the mountains.

"Hot damn!" Griffin yelled, once he was settled and bouncing along. "Don't drag your feet on the ground, Don Quixote! *Más rápido, Lobito.*"

The animals wouldn't go any faster. A ponderous jog was their top speed, yet they moved steadily, never balking. It was a fine way of traveling for awhile. There were no saddles or stirrups or other leather paraphernalia, but for the first few hours we were perfectly comfortable straddling the mats. Going uphill we held tightly to them, and going downhill we gripped the rope reins fitted to metal bits in their mouths. Except for the lead *burro*, no guiding was necessary, and Lobito's mount always led. We had it easy for the first six hours at any rate. All three animals were brawny and amazingly game, lugging us up the extremely steep trails all morning and well into the afternoon. Occasionally, when the going was particularly steep or the path particularly precarious, Griffin and I got off and walked just behind their twitching tails. Once we climbed that way for maybe an hour or more. It considerably eased their labor, but in the long run this proved to be a mistake, a bad one. The exertion proved too much for Griffin's ankle, and I felt it slowly draining away the slight reserves of strength we'd managed to regain.

Lacking that fine edge of stamina, we found it difficult to resist the force of the mid-afternoon sun. For that reason we were dizzy and truly exhausted by the time we reached a plateau from which we could see in the far distance the high pastures of what we presumed was La Plata. It looked to me to be about a two-hour ride. It was obvious the day's exertion had taken as much or even more out of the *burros*. Their heads were beginning to droop, their bodies were overheated and sweating heavily, and their breathing had become raucous by the time we began traveling through a fairly flat stretch of sugar cane.

The stalks were tall, more than six feet high, probably ready for harvest. Every time the *burros* snorted, a thick white foam emerged from their mouths and flaring nostrils. Motionless in the somnolent heat, the cane was a dull gold color, like bamboo, and it stretched on and on. A cloying, sweet odor hung thick in the air. We were following a path so narrow the rough cane leaves chafed constantly against our legs, just enough to keep us from dozing off, yet not quite enough to keep us alert. All three of us were in a sleepy stupor when suddenly Lobito halted his *burro*, flipped his *sombrero* back and stiffened upward to a rigid stance with his head cocked slightly to one side.

Griffin's *burro* stopped just behind him. Mine nudged up against Griffin's.

"What is it?" I asked. "Why are we stopping?"

Griffin shrugged, watching the boy. I watched him too. For another few moments he sat perfectly still. Then he jerked higher upright on his animal's back and, shading his eyes, stared over the shimmering cane to the left of us.

"What is it?" I demanded.

"Shut up!" Griffin snapped.

Finally I heard a distant, quavering drone and interpreted it as an airplane. That meant nothing to me. I realized it was getting closer, but not until more seconds had passed did it occur to me what this would mean to the boy. A split-second after that Lobito screamed at the top of his lungs.

"*Avión,*" he repeated in a shrill outburst of terror. Simultaneously he slapped his spurs into his *burro's* flanks. The startled animal plunged headlong into the cane.

"Lobito!" Griffin shouted. Yanking the reins, he shouted again and kicked his feet into his *burro's* sagging belly. It was the first time he'd used the single spur. That and the unexpected tug on the bit sent his animal charging into the cane. For a moment I was the only one still on the path. From my left came the sounds of Griffin's burro smashing blindly through the cane while he kept yelling, trying to get it under control. From my right at increasing distance came the noise of Lobito's charging *burro.*

And the growing roar of the plane itself. My *burro* tensed under my legs. I jumped off and whacked it hard on the rump. It bolted after Lobito's animal. I smashed ahead into the cane, moving toward the sound of the animals, but the cane stalks were hard and resistant. I had to hack at them with both arms to make any headway. When I jumped up to try to see Lobito over the cane, I saw the plane itself—swooping straight toward us, flying low, fire spurting from its wing-cannons. Small bombs or rockets were visible under each wing. I threw myself to the ground and heard a loud *pud-pud-pud-pud-pud.* The cane thrashed around me. When I picked myself up, the plane was already circling back toward us. Again I started after Lobito. The animals were barking out terrified sounds as they continued plunging ahead. I kept stumbling forward, hurtling through the stalks. Again there was the *pud-pud-*

pud-pud as shells tore into the sugar cane. Something Griffin had said—napalm—came to mind as I fell sprawling over broken stalks, gasping for air, coughing in the cane dust. Then the noise began diminishing. Holding my breath, I strained to hear as the sound of the plane waned to a distant quavering drone. It became so faint I could hear Griffin yelling from some far place in the field.

"Lobito, Lobito," he was screaming. "Paul!"

I scrambled to my feet and shouted in his direction over the crazed barking of the *burros*, "Over here! You all right?"

He didn't reply and I didn't wait for an answer, shoving through the cane, bashing it, coughing uncontrollably from the dust. Fast as I moved, it took several long minutes to find the boy's *burro*, standing shuddering in a circle of crushed cane stalks. Its eyes were wild, its stomach heaving convulsively. Shreds of cane leaves stuck to its foam-covered coat.

"Over here," I yelled. "You're getting closer!"

"Lobito with you?"

"No," I hollered, coughing. "just his *burro*."

That moment I noticed blood, wet blood, clots of it, just ahead on the cane stalks flattened by the *burro*. I pushed past them until I saw the boy sprawled in a sort of fetal position on the ground. For one awful moment I thought he was dead, but he was only extremely frightened. His face and arms were scratched badly, but he hadn't been hit. He wasn't crying, although he had vomited onto his shirt. I helped him to his feet. He held tightly to me until he pulled away to examine the deep wound on his *burro's* shoulder. I rubbed some of the sticky paste of dust and sweat and leaves from the *burro's* quivering flanks. Then Griffin came breaking through the cane, leading his animal by the reins. When he saw us he dropped the reins and just stood there, staring intently at us. All the noise had stopped.

"You're shaking," I said to him. "Help me find my donkey."

Lobito took hold of the dropped reins and pressed them into Griffin's hand.

"Okay," he said oddly. "It's okay. It's going to be okay."

He said something else to Lobito and the two of them mounted one of the *burros*, Griffin cradling the boy. I climbed onto the other one. Both animals resumed plodding in the direction we'd been going. Soon we saw in the packed dirt of the path a series of fresh holes and loose soil made by the strafing. The need to find my *burro* overcame the throbbing in my arms and legs, and somewhat checked the raw nausea I felt.

We were nearly out of the cane field when we came to my *burro*. We heard it first, then found it sprawled on the ground. From its throat came a horrible bubbling sound. With every spasmodic kick of one of its legs, more clotted blood spurted from its rear end. Yet more blood gushed from the wound that had splintered its back. The other *burros* wouldn't go near the dying creature. Lobito wouldn't look at it.

"Okay," Griffin muttered, handing Lobito to me. "All right. Take him away."

Griffin slid to the ground and walked over to the dying animal. When I looked back through the cane, Griffin had grabbed one of the donkey's long ears and was savagely kicking his heavy combat boot into the animal's head. There was a terrible sound. Both donkeys shied. In that glare of dusty sunlight Griffin kicked again, putting into each blow a furious power until the animal's legs stiffened spasmodically and stopped stirring, although Griffin kept kicking until the skull had caved in.

When we tried to settle Lobito on the larger donkey behind Griffin, he adamantly refused then relented, pressing his face against Griffin's back with his arms tightly around him. He clearly understood the need for haste, as well as the importance of finding cover. We didn't talk about what had happened. We didn't know if that pilot might have summoned another plane or called for ground troops to intercept us. I recalled a report I'd read back in New York that the US had jet fighter planes stationed in Cuba, supposedly for hemispheric defense, yet neither Griffin nor I had seen any markings on that plane.

9

April, 1958: La Plata, high in the Sierra Maestra

La Plata was a small and heavily overgrown plateau high on Pico Turquino, the Sierra Maestra's tallest peak. We arrived late in the afternoon. Only a few individuals were moving around among the various thatched *bohios* concealed among the trees and clotted vegetation. One *bohio* had a tin roof, while the others were constructed with wood planks below the ubiquitous thatching. We showed our press cards to the two rebels keeping watch. One wore olive khakis and a *26 de Julio* armband. They were crouched in the shade, working on a machine gun whose parts were spread on a tarpaulin. They said they were expecting us but their welcome wasn't particularly warm. They shook our hands with a certain reserve. They pointed out one of the *bohios* and said we could sleep there on hammocks until Fidel and the others returned.

Lobito immediately found a brush and pail of water and thoroughly occupied himself scrubbing down the *burros* and mules, all the while talking to them, murmuring directly into their hairy ears, calming them. We asked if he wanted us to help. He shook his head emphatically. We could tell he didn't want us to see he'd been crying. I was relieved a bit later when two other kids came whooping and laughing out of the trees to greet him and the donkeys.

Gradually more individuals appeared at the La Plata compound. In a small, drafty shack we came upon two rebels lying on cots, trying to sleep while awaiting the medicine and morphine due to arrive with the *Comandante*'s troop. One of them, Calixto, had been shot in the shoulder. Two bullets had been recently removed. The other was down with an intestinal problem. They were being tended by Haydée Santamaría, a woman in her thirties wearing trousers and a dark blue blouse. She had a broad, placid face, very maternal, that looked to be invariably comforting. Over the next few days we learned of her horrible history. Calixto had spent several years in Miami and loved speaking English. He informed Griffin that Haydée had participated in the daring but failed assault on the Moncada Barracks in Santiago de Cuba—the assault that gave the rebel movement its name, *26 de Julio*. That happened in 1953. Along with the others in this action, she'd been captured and tortured. Guards at the prison, Calixto told us, taunted her with the ripped-out eye of her brother Abel and threatened to bring her his other eye if she didn't provide them with information. It was also reported that other guards showed her a mangled testicle and told her it was from her fiancé's dead body. She refused to talk, and when finally released she became a leader in the rebel movement. Now she was in the mountains assisting Fidel's core group. Calixto told us he was very proud to be personally tended by the great Haydée Santamaría. When we asked her later about her political history, she was evasive, then politely dismissive, saying that she was merely another drop in the long river of Cuban history.

I thought of this every time I saw her, and I saw her frequently over the next few weeks, until she left, it was said, on a secret mission to raise funds. That first evening after supper we knew none of this. She was putting a clean dressing on Griffin's bad ankle before tending to my feet. With a very sharp hunting knife sterilized over flames on the cooking range, she gently sliced open each toe just under the nails, then squeezed out the pus, including appalling numbers of tiny white worms that washed out in the blood. After applying a stinging disinfectant and handing me clean socks, she even managed to find me a pair of old hiking boots, barely large enough to fit my swollen feet.

We often saw her working the water pump, making coffee, preparing food, as well as tending to incapacitated rebels, generally overseeing everything that was going on, even making sure Lobito brushed his teeth properly. We were told that Fidel and his troop were expected although they didn't know when. Haydée explained that the *Comandante* had learned never to reveal his plans.

As soon as we appeared each morning in the cooking shed, she would hand us tin cans, or sometimes small glasses, filled with thick black coffee sweetened with cane juice. She would then return to her chores, always finding time to greet the local folks who appeared every now and then with a few eggs or fresh vegetables, or batteries, cigarettes, candy bars, or other supplies easily carried. Many of the small settlements of *guajiros* scattered throughout the mountains were showing their support with these gifts. One of the rebels seemed always to be on hand to pay cash for all items brought. Often the *guajiros* refused to accept payment. One afternoon a shirtless boy about eight years old rode up on a palomino mare, leaned down from the saddle and unwrapped a burlap bag tied to the saddle horn.

"*Para él,*" he said to Haydée, "*adios, señora.*"

In the bag was an unwrapped chunk of crumbling white cheese, a can of condensed milk, and two long cigars in glass tubes. Another time a very old woman trudged wearily up to Haydée and handed her a little woven basket containing a ballpoint pen and three green turtle eggs.

"*Para él,*" she said.

We carried our coffee with us as we prowled around the hilltop, hoping to catch a glimpse of an approaching column of men. There were mountains in all four directions. Around midmorning we would amble with borrowed machetes down to the nearest stand of sugar cane. We hacked down the ripest stalks, which we dragged back to the cooking shed to be crushed into juice for the wounded and for general use. Having cut a few stalks for ourselves, we'd take refuge from the sun on the shadowy side of the veranda on crude handmade chairs. We spent long afternoons listlessly chewing lengths of cane into pithy wads, swallowing the sweet juice, spitting out mouthfuls of fiber, and dozing intermittently. There was no escaping the heat. From time to time the sound of an airplane jerked us to alarmed attentiveness, but the planes never came near. Usually it was so quiet we could hear the tarantulas rustling in the thatching above us. This too was a source of anxiety. About the size of my open hand and very hairy, they were sluggish but dangerous. According to Haydée their bite could paralyze a healthy man's arm or leg for days. Calixto told us that Fidel had been bitten on the arm by a tarantula and had lost the use of his arm for a full week.

When the heat diminished near sundown there inevitably rose the ache of hunger. There were inexhaustible quantities of cloyingly sweet sugar cane, and water could always be coaxed through the pump, but there was little food beyond small portions of rice and beans, or *malanga*, and occasionally an egg or bits of rabbit or chicken. The shortage of food led to our increasingly smoking cigarettes, something new to me. Tobacco was in abundant supply. Soon we were climbing into our hammocks or stretching out on the ground early in the evening, smoking, listening to Calixto. He told us how difficult it had been at first for the *26 de Julio* movement to achieve trust and good working relations with the people of the Sierra Maestra.

Most were illiterate. At first they openly mistrusted the rebels, but Fidel insisted on certain policies that showed the *guajiros* respect, even friendship. In time he managed to persuade them that his plans for Cuba would benefit them. He promised they would soon own the land their families had long worked as impoverished sharecroppers. They had never liked or trusted the army or the police, who habitually stole from them and often brutalized them. Gradually the mountain people came to understand that this battle was also their battle for a better life. Calixto said that some of the *guajiros* had even joined the rebels and were now carrying arms, as well as doing a great deal of the necessary work to supply the rebels.

Haydée warned us that when Castro did arrive he would probably be in a grim mood, as the recent general strike had proven to be a fiasco. Fidel had openly opposed a nationwide strike, she said, deeming it premature, but leaders of other groups had called for the strike anyway, and Fidel reluctantly went along with it. The Cuban Communist Party strongly opposed any general strike, fearing successful labor stoppage would only strengthen the 26th of July movement, their political rival. They sent out warnings to workers indicating they would permanently lose their jobs if they walked out. Batista threatened potential strikers with death, but the *huelga* nevertheless was called, and utterly failed in a strongly demoralizing setback. Despite his qualms about it, Fidel had hoped the economy might be crippled by work stoppages throughout the island, delivering Batista a strong rebuke. Due to its failure, fighting would now have to continue and in fact be stepped up. Haydée ended the conversation with a coy hint that she had a strong intuition we would soon be having visitors.

Although there was nothing discernibly different, I sensed a heightened air of anticipation in the cooking shed the next morning. People were moving around more vigorously. The first real sign came when Haydée, handing us our coffees, caught my eye and gave a positive nod. Fresh excitement flooded through me, and I realized what a huge amount of anticipation I'd been carrying. It was just after noon, the sun near its most intense, when we saw a thin column of dust rising just beyond a thicket of coffee trees below us.

We watched them approach: a file of some thirty men moving briskly uphill, moving roughly two abreast, accompanied by several heavily-loaded mules. At the head of the file, climbing with a powerful stride despite an immense backpack, was Fidel, taller and paler than I'd expected. Except for the eyeglasses, he looked like one of El Greco's patriarchs—that long, bearded face with heavy eyebrows and the profound expression of unfaltering earnestness. Rugged and muscular in baggy olive khakis covered with dust, he was carrying a rifle with a telescopic sight. Beside him strode a short, wiry woman, surprisingly small, yet managing to keep pace with him. We soon learned this was Celia Sánchez. As they drew near, her bright, raptor-like eyes appeared to be registering every detail of our features.

Haydée hurried over, clearly delighted to greet them. Fidel handed his rifle to Celia and took Haydée's round face gently between his hands. They looked intently into one another's eyes for a long, tender moment before she stepped back and turned to greet Celia. She did this very emotionally. It was clear they meant a great deal to one another. Then she introduced us to Celia and Fidel.

Celia greeted us each with a firm handshake and unmistakable concern regarding us.

"¡Los periodistas norteamericanos!" Castro said enthusiastically, "¡Qué jóvenes!"

"So young, yes," he added in English, "Eighteen, veinte. Pero fuerte, sí." His strong hands clasped my shoulders.

"Paul," he said, "it is my honor to meet you."

"No, *Comandante*," Griffin spoke up, *"es un honor para nosotros."*

"Ricardo," Castro responded, clasping Griffin's shoulders the same way. *"Bienvenidos, muchachos,* welcome," he said. "Later we will have a long talk together. I am pleased you have come. You will tell me all about yourselves, yes? "

His warmth and forceful presence were astonishing, certainly all I had hoped for and somehow much more. I was thrilled. While Fidel was only eleven years older than me, he seemed infinitely more mature, more developed, more worldly. His presence, while amazingly powerful, seemed to me completely unthreatening. Throwing one arm around Celia, the other around Haydée, he strolled away between them. More than a little awed, Griffin and I just stood there silently, watching them, absorbing the moment, then watching the men wriggle off their rucksacks and begin unpacking the animals. I was surprised to see how many sorts of hats they were wearing—from black berets to floppy straw *sombreros* to cowboy style felt hats and cloth baseball caps. Not one wore a metal helmet. All of them found places in the shade and some of them set about cleaning their weapons. Strikingly like the men I'd seen in that Movietone newsreel, there was a marvelous range of skin colors. One boy who couldn't have been more than fifteen had a Thompson submachine gun slung across his back. Several bearded soldiers in their late thirties or early forties were supervising, in a hurry to get all traces of their arrival hidden as soon as possible. Griffin and I helped carry gear and weapons into the cooking shed or into one of the huts.

Lobito appeared and hugged several of the rebels before leading the animals away. I joined a few of the men hanging makeshift hammocks of soiled blankets. Some of them smiled or nodded amiably to me, while others maintained a distance. I recognized one of the new arrivals as the rebel who had given us chocolate on that windy ridge days earlier. He greeted me again with genuine warmth. I tried a few phrases in Spanish. He replied in English as incomprehensible to me as my Spanish was to him. We simply couldn't understand one another, so we just shook hands and exchanged rueful laughs and backslaps and returned to our tasks.

"He was trying to tell you," said an amused voice behind me, "that he and his comrades destroyed a tank just outside Bayamo."

The voice belonged to a much older man, one with the most profoundly congenial face I'd ever seen. This was René Vallejo, a medical doctor and longtime personal aide to Fidel. He had amused brown eyes that sparkled with cheerful intelligence, a full salt-and-pepper beard, a high forehead, and a prepossessing air of pure amiability, perhaps like a Cuban Santa Claus. I took an immediate strong liking to him. Oddly, he appeared to be almost as interested in me. I decided to try to interview him soon. While we were hanging the last of the hammocks he told us he was not only the oldest man there, but probably the oldest member, at least in the mountains, of the entire *movimiento*. During the Second World War he'd been a medic, he told us, with the US Army in Germany.

"Yes," he said, "Thousands of Cubans served your country in that war, but I think it won't happen again, not like that. I don't know how much you understand, Paul, and I don't want to offend you, but the United States has been much too greedy since that war, and much too hostile. As many say, 'we love the American people, but not their government.'"

Griffin joined us. He and Dr Vallejo shook hands in a mutually appraising manner. I didn't see any of the immediate acceptance I had felt.

"You'll excuse me," the Doctor soon said. "Someone must supervise the butchering of the *burro*."

"We're eating *burro*?" asked Griffin.

"If the meat isn't spoiled," the Doctor replied. "The animal fell a few days ago. It was brought to us only yesterday. I look forward to talking with each of you later."

But he wasn't there when we gathered around a large table for supper with some of the men at makeshift tables nearby. Since early afternoon rebels had continued to arrive, mostly on horses and *burros*. An air of solemnity prevailed. While pouring glasses of water, Haydée paused long enough to tell us the Doctor had left for a nearby village to deliver a baby. She promised we would see him the next day. As for the meal itself, beans and *malanga* with tough chunks of charred *burro* were served with crumbs of the white cheese brought by the palomino rider. We both ate hungrily, not talking much, our mouths usually full.

At one point Fidel shouted to us from the far end of the long table: "*Muchachos!*" he called out, "The food of Oriente is tasty, yes? Much flavor! You are enjoying it?"

We responded enthusiastically. Fidel nodded acknowledgment and turned back to an intense conversation with the rebels around him, probably about the failure of the general strike. A heated discussion was in progress, and it went on a long time. I was surprised they all managed to keep their voices prudently subdued.

"It's not us," Griffin explained. "They're used to whispering. A couple of them don't want us here. We're *yanquis,* and they can't afford *gringo* spectators, food being so scarce."

"But Haydeé said Fidel *likes* talking to journalists," I said. "He thinks it's helpful to the movement. It improves their image abroad." We already knew that other journalists, mostly European, had visited this mountain stronghold earlier. We knew about Herbert Matthews.

"Quiet. Let me listen."

For a good while I watched Fidel. Everyone listened to him with remarkable attentiveness. He maintained a fervor so dominating it looked to be captivating each person. I studied the faces of Fidel and Celia and Haydée and a few of the other leaders, all huddled together in the light of a kerosene lantern. Even though I couldn't understand their words, I felt I could read their expressions and even intuit some of their thoughts. In reality, of course, I couldn't do either, so I kept urging Griffin to tell me what they were saying. Nevertheless, I got a strong sense of the depth of solidarity shared even during the fiercest arguments.

"It's basically about the failure of the *huelga*, the strike," Griffin explained. "It's an enormous issue. They're criticizing certain leaders and even redistributing zones of authority. A huge power shift is happening. The *huelga* failure provoked a major break between various revolutionary groups, particularly between those in the plains and those up here in the Sierra."

"Because other factions opposed a strike?" I asked.

"I don't think so," he said irritably, clearly tiring of translating.

At the other end of the table Haydée slid a cigar out of a glass tube and handed it to Fidel, who set it alight with great relish.

"You know," Griffin said, "it's difficult to think of her as a rebel, a fighter, Haydée. She looks so much like one of those bourgeois women that played bridge with my mother. I've been wondering how in hell any woman could go through all she has and not show it."

"According to Calixto," I said, "she has burn scars over most of her body. She keeps them hidden. And she doesn't discuss it."

At that moment, René Rodríguez entered and set a battery pack and a long-range receiving set on the table in front of Fidel. Lithe and handsome, friendly, about my age, René had startled me early that afternoon. In spite of a sleekly trimmed beard he looked almost exactly like the hotshot second-baseman on the American Legion team I'd played for in Pittsburgh. When I'd mentioned this to him, he'd told me he not only loved *beisbol* but in fact did play second base. It was a joy that René spoke English and was so sociable. He'd lived in the United States for several years, as had a surprising number of the rebels. Known fondly to Fidel as *El Flaco* (the skinny one), he was one of Fidel's chief aides. He spent a few minutes adjusting the antenna and fiddling with the dials before the radio crackled into action with Cuban dance music. Fidel played with the dial again, finally settling on a Havana news broadcast concerning the results of a violent raid the night before. A government spokesman was proudly announcing that the army had triumphed in every way possible, and all the criminal rebels had been killed.

"*Muchachos*," Fidel called to us. "I am sorry. I wanted you to hear our *Radio Rebelde*. It is our own short wave channel. It broadcasts authentic news, news that has truly happened, not the fantasies of the insane dictator. It is good, I think—our *Radio Rebelde*—very good. Yes, but this night I believe it must be said in truth that it is not very good."

Early the next morning it looked as though some of the rebels who arrived yesterday were already gone or leaving. Two small groups were setting off on foot. When we carried our coffees outside, looking for a place in the shade, Celia stopped us. I was struck again by how small she was, how short and how perpetually alert. The smallest uniform seemed too large for her. She took a cigarette out of her mouth long enough to ask if we could provide her with some information. She said this in a way intended to elicit instant agreement. Griffin translated as she went on, "Fidel is fully occupied with our work, but he is willing to be interviewed. It is very important for us to be portrayed in the United States with fairness and honesty. You understand? Is it possible for us to read some of your previous reporting?"

Griffin looked at me. So did Celia. Clearly she was all business. The look in her eyes was penetrating and persistent. I was flustered.

"I'm sorry," I finally said. "We didn't bring anything. We thought it was safer that way. If we got searched, I mean."

"Ricardo has accompanied you to translate?"

"Yes, and to take photos," I said.

"He is employed by the same newspaper?"

"He's more freelance," I said. "We didn't know what to expect. We just hoped . . ."

Celia impatiently shook her head and blew out smoke. There was a kind of barely restrained ferocity about her. "Fidel must keep moving," she said sternly. "It is very rare for him to sleep in the same place for two nights in a row. We must keep moving. It is extremely dangerous for us. Airplanes are bombing villages now all through Oriente. They are sending columns into the mountains to kill us. It's a new offensive. We are very short on supplies. Food and medicine are scarce. Do you understand?"

I nodded uncertainly, wishing we hadn't accepted the coffee. This was awkward. It never occurred to us that Fidel might be constantly on the move.

"How old are you?" Celia asked me.

"Twenty," I replied. "Ricardo is twenty-four."

"How will you return from these mountains? How will you travel back to New York?"

"We're not sure," I said. "We haven't thought about that yet."

She wasn't pleased. She took a final drag on the cigarette, then bent down and pushed it into the ground before straightening back up to grind it thoroughly with her boot.

"We have many severe difficulties," she said, looking from me to Griffin and back again. "We cannot accept you two as our responsibilities. We are making a revolution. You cannot be a problem for Fidel in any way. Do you understand this? You cannot be any burden for this revolution."

We each nodded. I hoped I didn't look as miserable as I was feeling. Much of it was chagrin. We hadn't considered how we might return. Nor had it occurred to either of us that we might prove to be nothing more than unwanted burdens.

"I will speak with Fidel," she said decisively. "But I must tell you something. It is clear to me that you are not professional journalists. I am astonished you managed to get here. There are now thousands of soldiers scattered all through these foothills. It is truly fantastic that you are here. But exactly *why* are you here? Fidel says he understands this. He is not troubled about it. He believes your intentions are sincere."

* * *

It was the drowsy middle of a steamy morning. Fidel was sitting outside with Dr Vallejo. They were both propped against a large tree that offered ample shade. Fidel had just finishing cleaning his rifle. As we approached, he gave it a few final strokes with a bore rod and an oily cloth before gesturing for us to sit down.

"We don't have enough rifles," he said. "This is a serious drawback. Because of this, it is of primary importance that we maintain each weapon in optimal working condition."

"Entiendo," said Griffin, dropping down to sit cross-legged near the two of them. I did the same. Fidel looked at him for a long moment and said, "You have been translating for Paul. I have seen this. How is it you know Spanish?"

"My early years were in Puerto Rico. I was born there. I still speak Spanish with my mother."

"And your father?" asked Fidel, "He is not Puerto Rican?"

162

"No, *señor*. Or do you prefer to be called *Comandante*?"

"I prefer Fidel. We do not use formal titles in the *movimiento*. I will call you Ricardo, yes?"

Griffin nodded affirmatively.

"*Bueno*, Ricardo, I understand you and Paul are *periodistas*, yes? The two of you are reporters working for the *New York Tribune*?"

Involuntarily Griffin glanced at me, then nodded at Fidel.

"*The New York Herald Tribune*," I spoke up. "The second biggest daily newspaper in New York. I'm hoping it will publish our interviews with you and some others here, like Haydée and Dr Vallejo. Maybe even Calixto."

"And Ricardo," said Fidel, frowning at me, "he will translate these interviews for you?"

"Yes. And he'll take photographs—with your permission, of course."

Fidel nodded slowly and said, "For the newspaper, yes? The one in New York that is not the *New York Times*? The one that assigned you to come here?"

Suddenly I had a strong hunch that he knew we were not professional journalists, let alone foreign correspondents. Celia had indicated as much. I felt deeply uneasy.

"For the *Herald Tribune*, yes," I said nevertheless, hating myself for trying to maintain this fiction.

"Fidel," Griffin spoke up, "Since we're not certain what topics might be out of bounds, maybe you can let us know as we go along."

Fidel kept watching me intently as I pulled out a ballpoint pen, readied it over my notebook and clicked it. When I looked up, our eyes met. At that moment I was certain he knew. He had to. A glance at Dr Vallejo, smiling sympathetically, provided further assurance.

"Perhaps," Fidel said, "you will first tell me something about yourselves. I am very interested that you are here. It is such a very long journey, no? And such a difficult journey. You have come all the way from New York to Cuba and then all the way into the Sierra. Haydée tells me you have no suitcases, no typewriter, no tape-recording machine. This is very unusual. Other journalists have come here, even foreign journalists. However, they have always made contact with the *movimiento* in advance. This has been true every time."

"Then they must have known how to contact the *movimiento*," said Griffin. "We didn't know how to get in touch. We're hoping to get good interviews."

Celia approached and called to Fidel. He beckoned her to come closer. She did, and briefly spoke to him, too quietly for us to hear before she returned to one of the huts.

"*Bueno*," Fidel resumed, turning again to Griffin. "Ask your questions."

"How many fighters do you have now?" asked Griffin. "How many men are presently in the 26th of July Movement?"

"How many *men*?" said Fidel, "Or are you asking how many fighters? I say this because many of our *combatientes* are women—like Celia, as you can see."

Griffin frowned.

I spoke up. "How many *individuals* do you count on to combat Batista's entire army?"

"Thousands," Fidel said promptly. "Tens of thousands. Hundreds of thousands. I count on all the students and artists and all the young workers, men and women—all the Cuban youth. They are all with the *movimiento,* although some of them do not yet fully understand this. Most of our youth, it is true, already understand clearly the politics of the revolution. They are ready to die for *la patria*. I promise you the masses are ready, not just the young. We have many seasoned fighters. We have substantial underground units in every major city."

"Isn't that wildly optimistic?" Griffin interrupted, clearly challenging him.

Fidel paused for a long moment, assessing him.

"You should know," he finally resumed, "that what is measured in the battle for freedom, for justice, is not the number of *combatientes,* as you asked me, Ricardo, but the number of virtues in the people. I can assure you that a single committed youth, one only, is worth one thousand ordinary men. The most arduous task for us, the most timely task for us, is to find these committed youths and prepare them for our decisive final drive. We have been multiplying our forces by strength and by discipline. All of us are anti-Batista. Even those intellectuals in Havana—"

"*Por favor,*" I interrupted, "could you please speak more slowly?"

"Of course, Paul, *ciertamente,*" he replied.

I was concentrated on scrawling key words as rapidly as I could when I glanced up and was shocked to see Griffin making an odd, comical face, clearly mocking Fidel. This jarred me. I was relieved Fidel hadn't seen him, but I wasn't at all confident the Doctor hadn't noticed.

"We must always have our feet planted on solid ground, of course," Fidel went on, "but we never sacrifice our principles, *nunca.* Our program must encompass all the serious economic problems confronting Cuba. None of us have illegitimate or unworthy ambitions. We cannot be selfish. We will be faithful, all of us, to our shared ideals until the final breath."

Griffin was looking at me with a challenging expression when Celia returned with glasses of black coffee for Fidel and Dr Vallejo. Fidel drank half of his straight down. Dr Vallejo sipped at his.

"Celia," Fidel said, "is very important to us. She has remained behind to discuss strategy with me. Some of the rebels have already left for the *emboscada* . . . yes, *emboscada?*"

"Ambush," the Doctor suggested.

"Yes, exactly," Fidel said, "another squad of Army soldiers are entering the foothills directly below us. This afternoon the rest of us must depart. Will you be marching with us?"

"We would very much like to go with you," I said, "provided it is all right with you."

"You understand the *movimiento* cannot be responsible for your safety?"

Both Griffin and I nodded that we understood.

"Fidel," I said, still wanting to get down more of the interview, "what would you say are the primary causes of so much poverty in Cuba?"

"This is a good question, Paul. It is a very good question. I will tell you the short answer, and then I must leave. It is basically the United States, the control of our economy by the United States. It is Yankee imperialism. It has profoundly corrupted our government. We will continue this conversation later."

Griffin had gotten up and moved around the tree to stand directly behind Fidel. He was doing facial antics again. I was appalled at these inexplicable attempts at distraction. I wanted to take in every one of Fidel's words.

Fidel turned to watch a very old man in a *sombrero* and soiled white shirt slowly approach. He was barefoot, using a cane, but still limping. He had a dirty patch over one eye. He carried a wet burlap bag."

"*Hola,*" Fidel said, "*que tal, hombre?*"

The man didn't seem to hear him. He came right up to us and with a big toothless grin extended his bag to Fidel.

"*Un regalo para tí,*" he said. "*Gracias por todo, Fidel. Muchas gracias por todo. Tengo ranitas.*"

"He brought a gift," Dr Vallejo translated for me, "Frogs. He has little frogs."

Fidel peered into the bag, then rose and bending over, gently embraced the man, who soon turned and started limping back down the path.

"*Sí, ranitas,* little frogs," said Fidel. "Last week he brought us a snake. We ate it the same night chopped into the rice. This *viejo* understands many things. I spoke with him when he brought the snake. He is alone. His wife is dead. He wants to do all he can to help us."

"Why did he hurry away like that?" I asked.

"Paul," Fidel said, clapping my shoulder, "you are observant and you are thoughtful. He left rapidly because he thought we were having a meeting of importance. He did not want to intrude on us."

"Fidel," the Doctor said. "We should be leaving now," Dr Vallejo intruded. "Celia wants us to get started now. You two will travel with us."

Griffin looked at me and shrugged. It seemed there was no choice. We would now do as we were told. Haydeé remained at La Plata with some half dozen rebels, including Calixto and the other *compañero* that was not yet recovered. Griffin and I grabbed our bags and soon were part of a group moving north through thick, tangled woods. Celia had found an old army canteen for us. I filled it with water and stuffed it into my bag. I was trying to avoid Griffin until my anger could subside. Basically I was feeling good about getting on paper some notes for an initial interview. I wanted to discuss it with Dr Vallejo but he was accompanying Fidel, who was on foot, leading the way, setting a brisk pace.

The clouds overhead were turning darker. An increasingly strong wind began blowing through the trees, tossing around vines and branches. We were on level ground, possibly an old game trail, when rain suddenly began falling with torrential force. There was no lightning, no thunder, just the loud pounding of a peculiarly warm downpour for maybe ten minutes. Then it stopped and the sky lightened to a luminous gray, leaving everyone soaking wet except for the few who'd been carrying ponchos. Many of us had cupped our hands to slurp down captured rain.

The path was now sopping wet clay and slippery roots and rocks. My boots were soon heavily caked with clay. When I stopped to scrape some of it off on a large rock, Griffin paused beside me.

"You're pissed off," he said.

"I'm very pissed off. Why the hell were you mocking Fidel? What was that about? You want to get us thrown out of here? I'm guessing Dr Vallejo saw those jackass antics of yours. What was that all about?"

'You really don't know?"

"I really don't."

"Okay," he said, "For the sake of argument, let's say I might have been guilty of a questionable response to him, but . . . you didn't feel that Fidel was insulting us?"

"Insulting us? Hardly. He's letting us accompany him!"

"Think about it," he said. "We're trying to do a serious interview. Fidel just spouts platitudes at us, as though we were back in college."

"He's giving us his idea of the big picture," I retorted. "It's just a start. There was no time for more questions. Why are you suddenly so damn antagonistic?"

"And why the hell are you sitting there taking dictation like some stupid secretary? We're supposed to be reporters. We're not part of this movement. We don't have to lap up all that rhetoric of his. We need to be asking hard questions. Can't you see that? Jesus!"

"You can't just start asking hostile questions. I was really moved by what he was saying. You were too busy being a jackass to even listen." I heard my voice rising and quickly lowered it. "I thought Fidel sounded like a leader should sound, an authentic revolutionary leading a necessary crusade, putting his life on the line for others. Do you realize how lucky we are to have gotten this far? To have his personal attention? I was ashamed to be with you back there."

He stared at me with an expression of absolute incredulity. Several rebels edged past us on the trail. Griffin didn't move. His expression didn't change.

"Know what I'm looking at?" he finally asked.

I didn't respond. I just stared back.

"I'm looking at a man who has discarded his critical faculty," he said. "A man who's suddenly become a true believer, a voluntary simpleton."

Dismayed, I shook my head and kept my mouth shut as I started walking faster, leaving him behind. I was shaken. Did this mean Griffin was entirely oblivious to the deeper spirit of the *Movimiento 26 de Julio*? Had I misjudged him that badly? Confused and hurt, I lit a cigarette. We stayed pretty much apart the rest of that long hike. It continued until many hours after dark. I had the canteen. Griffin would have to catch up to me if he wanted any water. At some point the moon came out, casting a helpful glow when we left the trail to follow a small creek up another hill, then across an overgrown meadow thick with wet bushes packed with protruding thorns. I hoped Griffin's ankle was holding up all right. I was almost certain my boots were already full of blood. This got me thinking about the others, the rebels, about their stamina and the resolve needed to keep on going and doing all the work entailed in setting up campsites and breaking them down, frequently engaging in battle, undergoing all the rigors requisite to waging this guerilla war. It quickly reduced any concern about my problematic feet to a proper perspective.

That night we stopped around midnight in another small hillside settlement of a few *bohios* and what smelled like a tobacco drying shed. The *campesinos* who lived there—it seemed like three families—were wonderfully accommodating. They seemed to know we were coming and roughly how many we were, as they had already prepared a meal that was awaiting us. I located Dr Vallejo and sat beside him on a fallen tree trunk in the night mist while we ate. He was entirely reassuring. Talking with him was a relief, partly because his English was so fluent, partly because everything he said made sense to me. Forking down what they called *bacalao,* salted codfish chopped into the seemingly inevitable *malanga,* he asked about my life. I described working in the steel mill and going to college. As I told him about Anna and her death, I was relieved that I didn't get all teary. When I described the newsreel I'd seen in New York about M-26-7, he was particularly interested to know exactly how the film had portrayed Fidel.

He thought Fidel would be interested in this, and in my own history as well. I felt flattered. He told me about his service with the US Army in postwar Germany, running a hospital for the sick and war-wounded. There he had met a Ukrainian nurse who had been in a Nazi forced labor camp. They'd gotten married before returning to Cuba and settling down in Oriente Province.

Dr Vallejo had left a successful medical practice and with both of his brothers gone into the mountains to join Fidel. He soon become Fidel's personal doctor as well as close friend. He spoke quietly about his own devotion. He explained what a profound honor he'd felt it was to serve the *Movimiento 26 de Julio.* He had absolutely no reservations about it. I didn't tell him about the sudden disagreement separating Griffin and me. He told me more about Guevara, the physician from Argentina whom he greatly admired, and about Juan Almeida and Camilo Cienfuegos, both of whom were leading small combat units in lowland areas north of the Sierra Maestra. He explained that Fidel's brother Raúl was leading a group of combatants in the Sierra Cristal, and that Guevara was in that group. It came as a happy surprise when, just as I was sinking into utter exhaustion, Celia appeared with a blanket for each of us. They were dry and heavy enough to ward off the marauding mosquitos.

10

)

Later in April, 1958

Fidel was involved in a strategy session during yet another
rain squall. He was seated at an outdoor table under a large
sheet of plastic hung taut between three trees. Celia and
two rebels I didn't know were huddled with him. The
Doctor and I were crouched under suspended ponchos, our
conversation muffled by water dripping all around us. He
was telling me about the Batista regime's crimes
throughout the island, but particularly the police and
military crimes in Oriente Province. He said that one of
Batista's most dangerous allies was Cuban Senator
Rolando Masferrer, basically a gangster who worked with
army officers and personally controlled a militia that
helped enforce Batista's repression. Civil liberties were
suspended throughout Oriente Province. The jails were
packed. Dr Vallejo assured me that Griffin and I had been
extraordinarily fortunate to get into the mountains. The
Bayamo area for many months was one of the worst locales
on the island in terms of young people being seized in
cafés, bars, markets, or on the streets. They were jailed,
tortured, and often killed. The regime was responsible for
thousands of political murders.

When he asked if I knew any of this before leaving the
States, I told him we knew very little beyond Herbert
Matthews' articles in *The New York Times,* and that
newsreel I'd mentioned. The Doctor told me, as had Celia,

that aerial bombardment in the mountains was intensifying, including the frequent use of napalm. Most of the victims were *guajiros*. Batista's soldiers routinely stopped the local people, often torturing them to elicit information, often killing them and leaving their maimed bodies near burned *bohios* as warnings for others. One result had been that more and more of the local people were helping the rebels, even enlisting as combatants, both men and women.

I confided to the Doctor that I hated the thought of being a drain on their meager resources, adding that I fervently hoped he would let me know how I might be helpful. I assured him I was a poor cook but a perfectly competent water carrier and wood hauler. Dr Vallejo chuckled, squeezed my knee, and promised he would let others know of my request to be given chores. He told me I might make myself useful by listening to Fidel and answering his questions about the United States. Because Fidel no longer went out on missions, the Doctor told me, he had a bit more time—only a few weeks earlier a number of rebels, including other leaders, had composed an eloquent letter urging him to cease participating in combat, to cease endangering his life, to do this for the good of the movement. Fidel was an outstanding fighter, the Doctor said, but the group letter convinced him to accede to their request.

"But he carries a rifle when we travel," I said.

"Yes," he acknowledged, "we could be attacked, but he stays back from the planned actions. We insist on this."

When René summoned the Doctor to join a strategy session with Fidel, Celia, Juan Almeida and a woman I hadn't seen before, I went looking for Griffin and finally found him sprawled alone on the ground, on a poncho, absorbed in reading a map.

"Want to see where we are?" He greeted me jovially. I was relieved he seemed happy to see me. Many times we'd gone over our situation and why I thought he needed to be respectful of Fidel. Griffin reluctantly agreed that our position was such that we should not be provocative. He moved the map and pointed to a spot on it. "Right here. Approximately, that is, above Santiago de Cuba, on the coast. Off to the east there, that's Guantánamo."

I settled beside him, trying to get some of the poncho under me.

"Where'd you get the map?"

"Borrowed it from Celia. She was willing to give it up when I told her I wanted to figure out a reasonably safe way for us to get down out of the mountains. She shook her head, of course, but finally lent me the map. I mentioned that I could use a better camera and she gave me a crappy little French Brownie left by a French reporter, with two rolls of film. I begged her to get us some more film."

"Did you figure out a way back to Bayamo?"

"There's no way back," he said. "We're stuck here, the army's been mining the foothills, posting entire regiments of troops. Last night a landmine just outside Bayamo blew up two locals. They were bringing supplies into the hills. A messenger told Fidel last night. Celia was sure this had never happened before. One of them was a girl."

"What kind of government," I asked, "places landmines in their own country?"

"A government under attack by its own citizens."

"It's grotesque. Did you interview Celia?"

"Nah," he said. "She's way too busy. She did ask if we'd help them with some work tomorrow. She expected me to agree right away. I told her I'd talk to you about it. It's not something I'm eager to do."

"What work?"

"They're expecting a small plane to land tomorrow at dawn a few miles from here, a friendly plane, bringing supplies, weapons. Most of the fighters are on other missions and won't be back in time. Celia wants this plane stripped of all ID as soon it lands, so the army won't know where it came from."

"I'm game," I said. "I've been wanting to help out."

"Think about it," Griffin said. "Do you really want to get involved to that extent? It's way the hell outside our job description. Journalists don't strip airplanes."

"Don't make it so complicated," I insisted. "It's simple enough. They need help. It's something we can do. What's the problem?"

He shook his head. "Think about it," he repeated, returning to study the map. "Don't make decisions like this without serious consideration."

"Why do you need to be so patronizing?" I responded.

"Listen, Paul, don't you want to be able to travel? In the future, I mean."

"I'm travelling now," I said. "Or do you call this something else?"

"To South America," he said. "Or Africa or China. To Europe. Anywhere you might need a passport?"

I didn't answer. I just looked at him and waited.

"The State Department can refuse to give you a passport," he said curtly. "Did you even know that? Get involved with the military of a foreign country and you'll soon find out. That's why I'm telling you to think this through. Do you really want to do war work?"

* * *

Rain continued falling in a relentless drizzle, as if a giant cloud swollen with water had settled down permanently over the mountain. We were all smoking in the dark after a late supper of rice and beans with bits of codfish, when Celia began rounding us up to brief us for the airplane mission. We would leave just after midnight and hike through rough terrain to the meadow where, at first light, the plane was expected to land. We would be in place

174

before dawn. I felt relieved when Griffin appeared beside me just as we were about to leave. I gave him a welcoming slap on the back and we started off. His limp was nearly gone. It felt good to be hiking with him again. I asked why he had changed his mind about taking part.

"Someone has to look after you," he said. Several strides later he explained, "Celia can be incredibly persuasive. When I told her my concerns about the government taking away my passport, she just shook her head and said she must have been wrong to think I was more than some shamefully timid *yanqui*.

It was still raining when we reached the landing site. There was worry that the sea of mud and coursing rivulets of water might prevent a safe landing. The local *guajiros* had already spent hours clearing away bushes and other botany to create a sufficiently wide runway through the meadow. We were given flashlights and lanterns and told to stand in two rows some twenty feet apart, and be prepared to hold our lights up like beacons as soon as the signal was given that the plane was approaching. By the time we were in position, the rain had ceased. We were soaking wet and having difficulty keeping our cigarettes lit. It was still dark. Gradually a warm breeze began blowing across the meadow. Pale pink light became visible on the eastern horizon, slowly spreading across the sky. We strained to hear an engine but heard only dripping sounds and the dawn twittering of birds. Another group of rebels appeared with six mules. They stopped in a thicket of trees at the meadow's edge and waited, lights ready, until at last it came—the distant sound of an engine growing louder until all at once there it was, dropping down expertly at the far end of the meadow, then bouncing and skidding noisily over sodden weeds and muddy hummocks of grass. The bright silver bulk of it caught the sunlight momentarily before the two engines went silent, and the plane shuddered to a halt with only a few feet to spare.

The pilot swung the door open and dropped to the ground amid calls of welcome and quiet applause. We were told later that he was a Cubana Airlines pilot. Nicaraguan students had loaded the plane with arms. We watched as the pilot began helping the other rebels haul the cargo off the plane and start packing it onto the mules. They worked hurriedly, swinging rapidly in smooth coordination and staying at it until the plane was empty. The cargo was mostly wooden cases of ammunition stenciled with a Beretta logo. There were also mortars and two machineguns. Then the rebels and some of the beacon holders vanished into the forest, leaving only four of us behind.

Our job was to remove all traces of identification from the plane's chassis, both the interior and exterior, and to do this at top speed—the plane's visibility from the air might bring an army patrol or an aerial attack. A rebel named Federico had screwdrivers and a metal pry-bar. Clouds of gnats began swarming furiously around us as we got started. They caught in our hair and eyes and stuck to the sweat on our faces and arms. We worked fast, prying off the metal plates welded along the fuselage and under both wings. The sky was turning a steamy bright white as the sun swelled. It was blistering as it reflected off the plane, heating the metal. Every surface we touched scorched us as we worked. Sweat poured off our bodies. The brightness and glare were almost blinding. It wasn't much better when we started on the interior, where there was no breeze to allay the suffocating heat. Federico used his machete to scratch off markings, and his cigarette lighter to burn off the numbers and letters stenciled on the plane, an astonishing amount of identification. A dark, lithe young woman named Violeta collected the metal we pried off and dropped it all into a burlap sack to be carried away and buried. She worked without pausing, whereas Griffin and I stopped every now and then to listen for approaching planes. When we finished, and each of us had double-checked that all insignia had been removed, we drank handfuls of rainwater from pools at the edge of the meadow before washing the sticky paste of gnats and sweat from our faces and arms.

Griffin walked beside me on the way back. Violeta was right behind us. She had a wonderfully spontaneous way of breaking out singing or suddenly humming aloud, yet softly. The first time I heard her, I applauded, until Federico signaled with a finger on his mouth to keep quiet. Griffin fell back and walked alongside her, all of us silent. I noticed once again how the forest seemed never to develop anything like permanent paths. Instead it seemed to close in again around us, sealing itself from intrusion.

* * *

I was jotting down some notes when Fidel ambled over, juggling three wild green oranges. The fresh supply of weapons and ammunition had him in a particularly exuberant mood. He asked if I played baseball. We were soon tossing the oranges back and forth while we walked and talked. Roughly the size of a softball, these oranges had pulpy skins covering small globes of acrid juice that was bitter to swallow yet provided energy and fresh clarity. Instead of bouncing when dropped, they often split apart. Fidel and I were tossing the last intact orange when we reached the *bohio* where the new weapons were stashed. Fidel balanced that orange on a tree limb, entered the shack, and emerged with one of the rifles, an M-1 Garand. It looked like the weapons I'd learned to use in ROTC. Motioning me to come with him, he moved back until we were some sixty feet from the orange. Shouldering the rifle, he aimed and fired off several shots before the orange exploded in a burst of juice and scraps of rind.

"You like to shoot?" he asked, extending the rifle to me.

I hesitated. "Not that much," I replied, briefly sighting the rifle before handing it back to him.

"My father took me hunting once, in Pittsburgh. I was just a kid. We went into the hills and he shot a young deer, although the kill shot could have been either of us. The whole thing ruined my sleep for many nights."

"Your friend said you have military skills."

"I had one year of army officer training."

Fidel nodded. "This was compulsory?" he asked.

"Sort of," I replied. "If I'd signed on for two years, I would've been enlisted in the army, expected to be ready to serve. I couldn't imagine doing that. One of my high school teachers had fought in Korea. He hated it. He said his unit never took prisoners, civilian or military. He told us he was ashamed of having served. It was the first time I'd ever heard anything like this from a war veteran."

Fidel waved to a squad of six rebels moving out on a mission. They waved back at us, so I waved too.

"They're incredible," I observed. "They always seem to be on the move, hurrying, never just walking, always pushing the pace. That kind of dedication is impressive."

Fidel agreed. "It's because we all share a single mission. We want to accomplish that mission rapidly, but prudently."

"Until you win," I said, surprised to see his immediate frown.

"The mission will continue," he admonished me. "Regardless of what stage it happens to be in, there is always room for more progress. Our revolution is international and eternal. It is never finished."

This puzzled me.

"At this point," he resumed, "Batista knows we are gaining support throughout the island. We are growing, we are improving," he said. I had my notebook out and was taking down all I could.

"The tyrant knows that Cuban people want much more than a simple change of government," he resumed. "They want radical change in every aspect of our political and social life. None of us will be satisfied with democracy in the abstract, such as you have in the United States. We are insisting on a decent living for every Cuban, which means education, medicine, employment and the opportunity to develop one's talents. This is what we are saying on Radio Rebelde, broadcasting across the entire island, telling every Cuban, even Batista's young recruits: 'Now is your time. Right now, this day, fight for this with all your might.'"

"I hope you will listen to our Radio Rebelde," he continued. "We discuss not only our triumphs but also our problems and our failures. We are honest. The people understand we are not perfect, we are flawed. Our message is credible to them. They listen to us until . . . they become us."

"I think I understand," I said.

"Paul," he went on, "it is very interesting to me that you have come here. I am not convinced you wish to be simply a reporter. I recall myself, my younger self, going to another country to join an armed struggle for justice."

He paused a long moment.

"I want to tell you that your CIA Director Allen Dulles visited Cuba three years ago to help Batista create a 'Bureau To Repress Communist Activities'. That is the official title. How will you write this for your American newspaper? It will not be printed. Your free press is not a free press. You must know this. Before we came to the mountains, even before Mexico, I traveled in your country up and down the East Coast. I met with hundreds of Cuban émigrés who had fled the repression here. I went to Bridgeport in Connecticut, to New York and Tampa. The émigré groups have been crucial in helping us financially. While I was there I saw how much your press is controlled by large corporations. These same corporations also control the economy here in Cuba, and in fact throughout Central and South America. Only five years ago your CIA deposed the democratic government of Guatemala. Did this, the terrible truth of this, ever appear in your press?"

"I don't know," I said guiltily. "I wasn't reading newspapers then. But is the American press really all that bad? It's true they glorify the United States. They keep repeating that we are the best country in the world, but sometimes they do criticize the government."

"And your friends, they understand this the way you do?" he asked.

I hesitated, thinking about it, while involuntarily noticing for the first time how the sun had turned the trees around us a lovely glowing lavender tone.

"Jacarandas," Fidel said, following my gaze. "Those are jacaranda trees."

"I don't have many friends," I finally admitted. "Griffin knows. The guys I worked with in the steel mill, they didn't trust the press—except for the sports section. Of course, I can only talk about guys I worked with, working class guys."

Fidel nodded. "Your working class has been a great success story," he said. "Thanks to labor unions, they have become a middle class. This is a triumph. Here it's very different. Cubans now have only one choice: either we endure this corrupt tyranny or we support the *movimiento*."

"That's good," I found myself saying. "It seems so clear, so necessary, and I'm deeply impressed by members of the movement here, Celia, Haydée, and Dr Vallejo and René. They're the finest individuals I've ever met. They're like you—smart and unselfish and devoted to a new and better Cuba."

"Yes, a new and better Cuba," he said approvingly, "and then of course a new and better world." Impulsively he hugged me with his free arm.

* * *

One morning when Fidel was alone, kneeling at a spring to fill his canteen, I waited for him to straighten up.

"Can I ask you a personal question?"

"Yes, of course," he said, twisting the cap back on.

"Do you believe in God?"

"I do," he immediately responded. "I was raised to be Catholic by my mother. From a very young age, however, I had deep concerns. There are passages in the Bible that troubled me. But why do you ask? Do you believe in a God?"

"Not the official Protestant god," I said. "Or the Catholic god, but I do believe in something . . . call it the sacred, although I can't define it as yet."

"Yes," Fidel said, "I don't believe in any personal god, or any god with a code of behavior. Just as you said, I believe in a positive spiritual force. You name it the sacred. Perhaps you are right. Of course, religion has no place in government, and absolutely no place in this revolution. Our revolution is entirely secular."

He twisted off the cap again and offered the canteen to me. I took it and had a good swig. So did he. The moment felt like a silent toast.

"From my reading," he then said, "I believe Jesus of Nazareth was a true revolutionary."

* * *

Griffin was doing exercises and dancers' calisthenics in the shade on a hillside with Violeta. They were accompanied by a rebel named Ciro, a college student from Matanzas whose two older sisters, he said tearfully, had been jailed for months and tortured by Batista's police. Ciro told us their only crime was chalking graffiti on the outer walls of a bank. He'd joined M-26 in hopes of eventually being able to kill his sisters' abusers. He was very intense, very likeable, although he didn't have any English. Griffin interrupted my feeble attempt at speaking Spanish with Ciro to tell me he wanted to do that night's hike alone with Violeta.

"I'm interviewing her," he explained, with nearly a straight face. "She's from Santiago. She wants to be a ballroom dancer."

"Be cautious," I warned him. "She's what? Sixteen years old?"

"No need to be concerned. Don't sweat it. Anyway, you've been preoccupied with Fidel."

He was right about that. I'd never met anyone even remotely like Fidel: he was so overwhelmingly confident that the future would be what he wanted it to be, so uniquely skilled at communicating this assurance to others. His friendliness toward me though, his unwavering candor and warmth, was somewhat bewildering. When I caught up to Dr Vallejo during the evening trek through the woods, I asked him about it. He said I should simply enjoy Fidel's friendship. He reminded me that he himself enjoyed a very close friendship with Fidel, as well as a profound sharing of the deepest ideals.

"But you're a medical doctor," I said. "You're a lot older than Fidel, with a great deal more experience. You're actually like a mentor to him."

Dr Vallejo laughed. He had a resounding, rolling bass laugh.

"Paul," he finally said. "Fidel likes you. Accept his affection and his interest. This is not something to be examined or to be worried about. I don't know if he told you, but when he was barely twenty-one years old, Fidel went to fight against Trujillo, the criminal dictator of the Dominican Republic. Shortly after that he went to Colombia, where he also involved himself in a rebellion. He's an absolute believer in the necessity of fighting against dictators anywhere on earth. It is a global mission to resist imperialism, to limit the rampant greed and oppression that is capitalism. I'm certain he is convinced that you share those ideals. He understands your engagement."

"Okay, Doctor, I appreciate your saying that."

"Please enjoy the opportunity," he said. "Fidel is offering you the purest, most important education one could possibly get. As you realize, he is a unique human being."

It was true that I was preoccupied with Fidel, yet whatever Griffin was up to mattered to me very much. Late that night our group reached a geographical area unlike any I'd seen. We'd been climbing downward in a column along a perilous cliff-side route that led to a ravine with a creek flowing through it. Filling our canteens, we continued from there, our route leading upward across a nearly bare hillside, almost pure bedrock, with a scattering of trees growing out of fissures in the granite. The sky, thick with bright stars, provided substantial light. The rock face, steeply angled, contained at least two caves. After several of the rebels examined the interior of the largest one with flashlights, looking for animals or snakes, we placed our packs and weapons inside the cave then tended to the two weary mules, lifting the heavier cargo from their backs.

Once they were tethered, watered, and fed armloads of grass, we settled down to sleep beside one another in the cave, or just outside near the entrance. Griffin had settled deeper in the cave. I was relieved to see he was alone, not with Violeta, yet it was bothersome that he seemed to be purposely avoiding me.

Celia announced there'd be no food until the next day, when *guajiros* were expected to meet us with provisions. I didn't hear a single complaint or groan of dismay. Canteens got passed around for sips of water and teeth brushing. Celia and Fidel had stretched out close to one another and were talking quietly. It wasn't unusual for us to go to sleep hungry and without cots or hammocks. Soon there was considerable snoring, and I decided to put off confronting Griffin.

* * *

Fidel loved eating. Typically we managed to have one meal a day. While he never mentioned it any of the many times I sat beside him, it was clear he deeply enjoyed whatever food was served. In times of extreme scarcity Celia always saw to it that he was provided with sufficient protein—an egg, a small slab of dried cod, a shard of some unidentified meat. He always chewed this thoroughly, savoring the flavor, extracting all the nutrition possible. No one ever complained about his occasionally getting more food. For instance, he was the only one who got *café con leche*—coffee with canned milk. We all understood the reasons for this. Even in our most selfish moods, not one of us wanted it any other way.

* * *

Morning light revealed the height of the rock face above us and the long vista of green hills below us rolling northward. The vines drooping down over the cave entrance were thick with orange blossoms attracting countless bees. The weather felt unusually fresh, rinsed, with the air still cool and the sun slowly making itself known. The news came by short wave radio not long after dawn. It was horrifying. A small army squadron had just raided Yarayabo, the settlement where Griffin and I first met Lobito—where the *guajiros* showed us such warm hospitality. Suspecting the *guajiro* families had been helping M-26, the soldiers summarily killed eleven people and left another four badly injured. Immediately Fidel sent

184

off eight rebels to engage with those soldiers. He estimated that by moving at full speed down the mountain, they could reach the settlement in roughly three hours. His orders were blunt: get there as fast as you can, kill the soldiers, assist the wounded *guajiros*.

As the shock of this news wore off, with the fate of Lobito still unknown, I felt a surge of raw anger. Those *guajiros* had been more than kind to us. I still felt grateful for the way they'd taken us in and prepared a feast for us. A few of their worn faces remained in my memory. I asked the Doctor if this sort of attack was a frequent occurrence. He said that only in recent months had soldiers begun making reprisals against anyone of any age suspected of collaborating. This was part of the new offensive they were all talking about. He also told me that besides dispatching the group of six, Fidel had sent several other groups from our unit to attack police stations and army vehicles in central Oriente. It seemed to me the M-26 was stretched extremely thin. Our conversation was interrupted then by several *guajiros* arriving on horses. They had baskets of food and cooking utensils, the provisions we were expecting. Assisted by several rebels, they set to building a fire with branches and the trunk of a dead tree hastily sawed into logs. A steady breeze dispersed the wood smoke, easing concern that the fire might be spotted from the air. Soon strong coffee was poured. Dried and fried *malanga* cakes were broken into chunks and passed around. As there were only three enamel cups and one tin can, those served first were expected to down their coffee rapidly so others could use the cups.

At the first opportunity I approached Fidel. He was giving instructions to Celia, who was writing them down in a pocket notebook. When he looked up, I apologized for disturbing them.

"Paul," Fidel said. "You have a question for me?"

"No question," I said. "A request. I want to do more. I want to help. I want to fight."

He didn't appear even slightly surprised. "You've thought about this," he said. "Have you discussed it with your friend?"

"We don't agree. Griffin has a different point of view, but I've felt part of this group, the movement, ever since we got here. Getting to know you and Dr Vallejo and you too, Celia, has only increased my feelings."

"But you haven't discussed this with your friend."

"I don't need his permission, and I certainly don't need his cautionary bullshit."

Celia nodded encouragingly.

"I've thought about my family, of course," I blurted, "and my American citizenship. They don't mean as much to me as this revolution does. I'm never going back to college. The opportunity to help means everything to me. I know you understand. You mentioned your respect for those Americans that went to Spain and fought in that civil war. I know I won't be any great help, but well, can't you use another fighter?"

Fidel slowly stroked his beard. He looked uncharacteristically noncommittal. I had a sudden stab of sheepishness hearing my own urgency, the raw immaturity of my voice.

Celia broke the awkward silence. "You need new socks," she observed, "and perhaps new underwear?" She had noticed my feet were sockless in the boots. "You have large feet, like Fidel."

"Let me speak with René about this," Fidel finally said pensively, offering his hand. "Thank you for your offer and your sincerity, Paul. Please understand that I do not take this lightly. As you know, we've recently acquired more weapons. Nevertheless, I would like to have El Flaco's opinion."

"When we return to La Plata," said Celia, "I will give you new clothing. For now, perhaps you would like to wash over in the *cascada*."

"The waterfall," Fidel said, seeing my confusion, pointing with an unlit cigar, "Just over there, beyond those rocks."

* * *

René had a 30-caliber carbine in his hands, and a longer rifle with a telescopic sight hanging from his shoulder. I asked him if Fidel had mentioned my request. He nodded and led me away from the others to a small stretch of stone bordered on one side by a thick cluster of trees. The top half of one of them, probably struck by lightning, tilted back to earth. When the trunk of it was about forty feet from us, René handed me the carbine and told me to put a few rounds into the tree at the height of a man's heart. I took a balanced stance, consciously controlled my breathing, and fired several single shots.

He shook his head. "*¡Hombre!*" he exclaimed, "Lower, lower. You know men whose hearts are ten feet high?"

The rifle needed calibrating but I didn't have a screwdriver. At least a few of my next shots hit the tree respectably lower.

"You need practice," he observed, retrieving the carbine. "But we can't waste more ammunition. Do you know how to fieldstrip this weapon? How to clean it?"

"I can fieldstrip an M-1. That's the only weapon I've ever used."

"That's good. Will you permit a few questions?"

"Of course."

"Have you ever been in combat?"

"Never."

"Have you ever seen combat?"

"No."

"Then listen to me. Combat destroys lives in many ways," he said gravely. "It can end your life. It can leave you helpless, in terrible pain for whatever remains of your life. In this way combat also destroys the lives of those who love you. Do you understand?"

"I think so. I've thought about this. My life doesn't mean—"

René broke in. "Fidel talks about the need for revolutionary change throughout the entire world," he said solemnly, "and he is entirely serious about it, but this war now, our civil war—this is a war for Cuba."

"And I'm not Cuban," I said.

He seemed pleased I understood.

"Neither is Ché," I pointed out. "He's from Argentina. I know that Fidel fought in the Dominican Republic. Maybe it's somehow significant that I wasn't born in Cuba, but I was born in the same world as you were, Fidel says this is a global war."

El Flaco leaned the carbine against the tree, then looked me in the eyes for a long moment before saying, "You already have some training. I regret we can't provide you more. That is our reality. We cannot."

When I nodded that I understood, he put both his arms around me and tightened them. It was *un abrazo fuerte*. A strong embrace.

"*Compañero,*" he said, "*bienvenido,* welcome to the 26 de Julio, hermano."

"*Gracias*, René. This is a great honor."

"I would like you to accompany me in our next action," he said. "I will oversee you. This is our routine."

I nodded my understanding.

Acceptance seemed even more certain a few days later when Celia brought me a heavily worn, slightly ripped backpack and a pair of faded old Levis. They were too big in the waist and too short, but I was glad to have them. The trousers I'd been wearing ever since our arrival in Cuba were torn and rotted beyond repair. I assumed her gift had to do with my now being a fledgling rebel, but no: she told me that Griffin had asked her to try to get some new clothes for me. When I told her that I had no idea how to pay for them, she just shrugged and handed me a length of old rope she said I could use as a belt.

The next few days, after a morning can of sweet coffee with a cigarette or two, I collected a few armloads of firewood before seeking out one of the rebels who could speak English, trying to find out more about what we were doing. I had no idea where Griffin was. I wanted to let him know that I'd enlisted. I knew that I should have talked it out with him before committing, but I didn't want to face his almost certain opposition. I wanted him to be with me in this. It troubled me that he wasn't.

Those rebels who now understood that I had volunteered did not change their behavior toward me. They remained basically indifferent rather than welcoming. Of course, they had no way of knowing whether I'd prove useful. I asked many of them about their own personal lives and their hopes for the future, usually with Dr Vallejo translating. Every one of them seemed confident we would win this war and bring social justice to Cuba.

11

May, 1958

The next time I saw René it was early morning, damp, clammy, still dark. He was leaning over me, with one hand shaking me awake, whispering that we had to hurry, *rápido, rápido*, we were leaving right away on an ambush. The mission was to stop a file of soldiers from climbing higher into the mountains. His other hand held a tin can of water. I cupped my hands and he poured the water into them so I could briskly wash my face and eyes. I hurriedly laced on my boots and found a tree to empty my bladder against. René was already leaving. An M-1 carbine with a leather sling on it was balanced on my backpack along with half a dozen clips of bullets. I pocketed one clip, shoved the others into the pack, grabbed it and the gun, and rushed to catch up. Calixto and an older rebel named Humberto were already walking at a fast pace behind René. The four of us left the grove of trees and started down a steep trail made perilous by the dew and the occasional loose rocks difficult to see in the remaining moonlight.

I was glad we were descending, yet concerned about my ability to keep up. Calixto and René, each carrying rifles, were agile as mountain goats, Humberto somewhat less so. Calixto cleared the thickest vine-tangled stretches with his machete, so we made decent time, never resting, until we came to a stretch of deep grass where there were several banana trees, a pen with chickens, some kind of vegetables growing in rows, and two *bohios*. René signaled us to stop at the edge of the woods and remain hidden. Calixto swiftly crossed the pasture to the larger hut and knocked on the front screen door. The second time he knocked, a shirtless *guajiro* stepped out and shook hands with him. They talked briefly before the *guajiro* went back inside and returned with a bunch of small yellow bananas. Calixto gave him some paper money. Again they shook hands.

Calixto hurried back, handing us each a banana. We ate on the move. They were small and overly ripe yet deliciously sweet, with the strongest flavor of banana I'd encountered. We stuffed the peels into our pockets. Humberto explained that the *guajiro* would have been alarmed and probably not opened his door had all four of us appeared.

We had probably been moving for three hours when René stopped us at the juncture of another trail, one likely made by animals, although there were human footprints as well, clearly visible in the morning light. It was a damp, mossy area where an underground spring kept the lower stretch wet and slippery. There were lots of tall ferns. The air smelled strongly of spearmint.

René signaled us to be silent. He kneeled down at the spring and filled his canteen. The rest of us did the same, cautious not to make noise. Humberto buried his banana peels under soft moss off to one side. We all did this. Then René spread his arms and drew Calixto and Humberto close together and spoke quietly in rapid Spanish, pointing twice in different directions. After nodding that they understood, Calixto started back along the trail the way we had come. Humberto ducked into the woods ahead of us. René motioned for me to come closer.

"We believe there are six soldiers in this unit," he said, his voice merely a hoarse whisper.

"Usually they advance in single file. They will pass here and probably stop for water. As soon as they come under fire they will separate and try to kill us. We'll be spread out and hidden, careful not to be in any of our own lines of fire."

"Okay."

"You should know that this particular army unit is part of a squadron that is known to have killed families of *guajiros*. The soldiers rape the girls and often the older women. Then they kill everyone."

"You're certain of this?"

"Yes. So is Fidel. We usually take prisoners, but these soldiers are not worthy of being prisoners. Is this clear? Do you understand?"

I nodded.

"Good. It is very important you understand this. Now, take cover up there on the hill, *hermano*. Make sure you have a clear line of fire to the spring. Do not shoot before I do."

I left him and climbed up through dense green shrubs to a small rise, where I found shade under a thick tree whose widespread tangle of roots splayed out above the ground. The other three weren't visible. I took my pack off and set it down. Lying across the roots and aiming the carbine, I had a clear view from one side of the tree down over a cluster of tall ferns to where the paths met. The aroma of fresh spearmint was even stronger here. I breathed deeply, feeling the mint begin to clear away traces of a slight headache. I wasn't afraid. I wasn't wondering—what if I'm shot in the stomach and have to go on living with ruined intestines? Part of my brain was turned off. I felt ready. I wondered if Fidel had assigned me this specific action with René so my first effort would be routine and maybe less dangerous. I wasn't a crack shot. I was certain the others were better. But I had skills. I didn't feel nervous. In fact, the sun and the hiking had me all too close to dozing off when I heard a new sound not quite like a birdcall and all at once several soldiers wearing camouflage helmets were standing below me near the spring. Others were coming into view. I thought I saw seven in all. Involuntarily I almost squeezed the trigger. Instead, I inhaled slowly, released the safety, and was aiming carefully at the middle of the chest of the tallest soldier when there was a terrific explosion in their midst—a grenade had detonated, dropping two of the soldiers and sending the others scattering. One of them came charging wildly up the hill directly toward me. I took aim and shot him twice, then once again as he was falling down. I scrambled to my feet and put another bullet directly into his chest before looking around to see that the rest of the soldiers had vanished. Two of them were killed by blasts from Calixto's shotgun. Another, retreating, ran straight into Humberto, positioned just off the trail waiting for him. René appeared at the spring and put a bullet directly into the forehead of each of the two soldiers felled by his grenade.

René and Calixto went rapidly through the soldiers' pockets, plucking wallets and pens and spare clips of ammunition. I considered taking a pair of boots to give Celia, but René stopped me, saying we had enough to carry back. We let the seventh soldier, if there had been a seventh, get away. René said that he would probably return to his battalion and let the others know how effective we'd been, or he would simply vanish, done forever with being a soldier. While the *movimiento* usually buried the dead, there was no discussion whatsoever about burying these particular dead, and there was no discernible air of triumph when we headed back. We were slowed by hauling the new weapons and ammunition. The heat had increased, and we were now hiking almost entirely uphill. We were sweating heavily. Horseflies had appeared. Despite our constant swatting at them, they kept biting us, leaving red welts that took days to disappear, provided they didn't get infected. We were also feeling the adrenaline settling down and our chemicals realigning. We were all solemn, not talking, just thinking about what had happened. I suppose each of us was at least a bit troubled and undergoing some inner turmoil.

* * *

One of the weapons we captured made Fidel particularly happy. It was a submachine-gun with a folding metal stock, very sleek. Fidel was boyishly eager to try out new weapons. When he left the encampment to give the captured gun a try-out, he waved for me to accompany him. We walked perhaps a mile to a clearing overlooking a valley. Beyond it was a vast panorama of hazy blue and green mountains.

"This is an American M-3," Fidel said cheerfully, holding it up for me to see. "Made in the United States by General Motors. Here's the logo. Your government supplies weapons and planes to Batista. We have officially tried to stop this, but we are ignored. More and more often now, we are capturing these weapons for our own use."

"But not the planes," I said.

"Not the planes, no."

"I don't think most Americans have the slightest idea what their tax money is doing."

"*El Flaco* tells me you're going to be a good soldier," he said. "He says you remain quiet under stress, you follow orders well, and you're a strong walker. These are valuable skills, Paul."

I felt a rush of pride. "Have you seen Griffin?" I asked.

"A few days ago, yes," Fidel said, "I saw him. He is doing useful work."

"Really? What's he doing?"

"He is working near Las Chivas, not far from Yarayabo. He is with Violeta. They're teaching children there, most of them survivors of the attacks. Some of them are orphans."

"Did he mention me? Did he leave a note?"

"I don't know, possibly. He was completely involved with the little ones."

"How long would it take me to get there?" I asked. "To Las Chivas?"

Fidel jammed a clip into the submachine gun, pointed it at the distant mountains, and started shooting. He emptied the clip in two deafening staccato bursts.

"Very effective," he said. "But only useful for close-in fighting." He ejected the clip and began refilling it, thumbing in loose bullets from his jacket pocket.

"Want to try it?" he asked.

"We shouldn't waste the ammunition," I replied, before adding hastily, "I'm not implying that you were, Fidel. Squandering bullets, I mean."

He laughed. "Perhaps you failed to see all the soldiers hiding in the shadows on that ridge. Is this possible? I have annihilated an entire regiment of the tyrant's army. Not one survivor. Be sure to write this down, Paul. A mere thirty rounds were fired by the legendary *comandante en jefe,* yet one hundred of the dictator's most vicious troops fell dead."

"Got it," I said. "And don't forget that fighter plane taken down by one of your shots," I said. "It crashed and blew up an army tank."

"No," Fidel said in mock reproach, "the plane you refer to, it crashed and blew up a tank *factory.* You must record this correctly. Objectively. This is what you saw."

"I did," I agreed. "I saw it with my own eyes. But the *comandante,* a profoundly modest man, down-played his part in all of this."

"¡Claro que sí!" Fidel exulted. "Write it this way exactly! At last, the truth, the *entire* truth, will appear in the *New York Times.*"

"How long," I asked him, "would it take me to get to Las Chivas?"

"Lobito's heading there. He can take you there tomorrow. Ride one of his *burros*, you're limping."

"Just blisters," I said.

"Don't let them get infected."

Celia and Dr Vallejo were waiting for him when we returned.

"Bad news," Fidel said to them. He was scowling. "This *yanqui* reporter here, he wasted many, many rounds of ammunition."

The Doctor chuckled. Celia looked displeased.

Fidel laughed and turned to me. "Be back in two days," he said, "the day after tomorrow, very early, and be ready to march."

* * *

I never got to Las Chivas, not then, not later. A different mission needed Lobito and his *burros*, so I didn't get to see Griffin for many days. Despite Fidel's remark, we didn't break camp as planned, although two groups did take off on undisclosed missions, and another group returned. *Guajiros* came often, sometimes bringing meager portions of food. We shared whatever they brought—a pot of cooked rice, a chicken, two dead snakes, an armload of greens, one time the bleeding haunch of a hog. We continued to smoke a lot. The smoke helped keep away the mosquitos and horseflies, as well as easing our hunger.

The heat increased as June advanced. The air became extremely dry. The sky was unclouded. I was glad of any shade. There was no mist, even at night. Every day I gathered armloads of firewood for the cooks, then refilled and hauled jerry cans of water from the creek, where we washed our clothes and ourselves. With a small can of oil borrowed from René I thoroughly cleaned my rifle. One afternoon I watched him make a hammock out of several burlap sacks and a length of heavy rope. When I admired his work, he insisted I keep the hammock, saying he had made it extra long in order to accommodate me. He added that he'd been concerned about my sleeping on the ground, easy prey to rodents and snakes and bugs. I was deeply touched by this. I wished I had something I could give him. We talked often. One day we noticed a great column of brown smoke rising from a hillside in the distance. The Doctor said several *bohios* were there next to a cornfield. Fidel trained his binoculars on the area but couldn't see any people, and we were too far away to be able to help. In fact, many of us were often preoccupied listening for airplanes. When I asked later about the smoke, no one seemed to know what had caused it. The *bohios*, however, appeared to be intact.

* * *

At first light we were going out on another ambush. This time René chose a recent recruit, Pablo, to accompany Calixto and me. Pablo carried a Remington .22, a lightweight rifle he'd been given on his twelfth birthday and had somehow managed to smuggle into the mountains. Pablo had been a second-year student at the University of Havana. Now nineteen, he seemed older. Like me, he'd had no guerilla training before going into combat. In excellent physical condition, he'd been a long-distance runner at the university. His father, an engineer accused of being a *fidelista*, was believed to be in prison, but this wasn't certain. Pablo said that his mother, a high school teacher, was a devout Catholic who prayed many times every day for Pablo and his father. The three of them once vacationed in New York City and visited Niagara Falls. He missed his parents and often talked about them, always with great concern and respect.

After an unusually cold and damp night, I woke with a queasy stomach. In frosty dawn light and without coffee, we set out moving single-file down steep slopes, through dense vegetation and across a shallow river with no overhead cover. We passed several small coffee plantations with beans spread out on raised platforms, drying in the sun. We were resting in a dense thicket south of a village when we were startled to hear male voices in a loud argument. They were getting nearer. Calixto took off running, holding his canteen pressed to his side so it wouldn't rattle against his ammunition belt. Soon he was back, whispering urgently to René. Five soldiers, he said, one with a machine gun on a tripod.

Following René's hurried orders, we separated and took cover in the brush before slipping off our backpacks and readying our weapons. Calixto headed off again, intending to position himself behind the file of soldiers. They were unbelievably reckless. Walking close to one another in single file, still arguing, all five of them came into clear view. The lead soldier was swinging a machete, clearing away vines. He had almost reached us when René stepped forward and opened fire, dropping him in his tracks. Calixto jumped into view on the trail behind the other soldiers, his submachine gun pointed at the sky. He fired off a burst. Immediately the second, third, and fourth soldiers dropped their weapons and raised their arms in surrender. The soldier carrying the machine gun hesitated but Pablo was on him, yanking away the weapon.

It all happened very quickly. Only two guns had been fired, yet suddenly we had four prisoners, each of them terrified. One was undergoing physical tremors, shivering with fear. Calixto and I kept our guns on them while René and Pablo bound their hands together with rope, removed their belts, and wrenched apart the buttons on their trousers, so the soldiers had to hold them up with tied hands or have their trousers fall down around their ankles. One of them started crying. Another lost control of his bladder. Apparently the army was sending its newest, least experienced men, and evidently they believed Batista's propaganda about Fidel's "vicious baby-eaters hiding in the mountains."

This method of ambush worked well many times. It required the army unit to be a small one, less than ten, moving in single file through heavy vegetation. You simply shoot the first man in the file and make it obvious you have the rear fully covered. Those soldiers who leave the path, bolting into thick brush, are easy to find.

* * *

One afternoon Celia walked past as I was scraping my fingernails rapidly back and forth on a granite stone that I'd pulled onto my lap.

"You don't have a fingernail clipper," she observed. "Is that method working?"

"Sort of. I don't know how it will do for my toenails."

"We have a clipper somewhere," she said. "I'll try to find it for you."

As she was always preoccupied, I was amazed she'd bother with such an insignificant chore.

"Would you like a haircut?" she asked me another time. She mimed cutting a strand of her own hair, using her fingers as scissors.

"*Sí, sí,*" I said. "*Muchísimas gracias.*"

12

June, 1958

I hadn't seen Griffin for nearly a full week when one afternoon I noticed him in the distance, involved in a conversation with one of the older rebels. While I think he saw me, there was no acknowledgment. I decided not to interrupt them. Later that same day two groups took off on undisclosed missions. At sunset the next day a group of five returned from yet another mission exhausted and upset. One of the rebels had been killed and another badly injured, men I'd often seen but didn't know. The entire camp received the news with a mingling of sadness and anger and renewed focus.

One afternoon there was a sudden commotion involving Fidel, Calixto, and a middle-aged *guajiro* I hadn't seen before. He was tied to a tree. He began screaming. Several of us rushed to quiet him. I was told Fidel had just accused him of being a collaborator. While readily admitting his guilt, the *guajiro* insisted that it wasn't his fault. He was saying, Dr Vallejo explained, that some kind of hairless animal had crawled into his ear and forced him to tell Batista's officers which of the *guajiros* were helping the rebels. He acknowledged that this information had led to deaths, but he blamed this on the hairless animal. He swore he had not betrayed our position. He begged Fidel to help him, or the creature would find its way into someone else's brain. Fidel appeared to be earnestly considering this when abruptly he turned his back and walked away, saying something to Calixto. Without hesitation Calixto moved backward a few steps, raised his revolver, and calmly shot the *guajiro* twice in the chest. As he lurched forward against the ropes, Calixto put a bullet into his forehead. A few quiet moments passed before several rebels stepped forward, untied the body, and helped Calixto drag it away. We left that campsite within hours.

* * *

I fell asleep resolved to talk with Griffin. Occasionally I'd seen him doing chores in the distance, or talking in a small group. More often I didn't see him for days. Was he still working with kids? I knew he was annoyed with me—the feeling was mutual, but I disliked the growing uneasiness. Putting it out of my mind didn't work. Then late one day I found him resting, reading a paperback mystery in Spanish that was making the rounds.

"Got time to walk a bit?" I asked him. He folded a page in the book, stuffed it into his bag and we set off walking.

"How are you?" I said, "I've been wondering what you've been doing, what you've been thinking."

"Really?"

"Yes, really."

"Since you're interested," he said, not looking at me, "what I'm thinking is that we're stuck here. We're completely stuck. It's like we're in limbo. There's no way we can leave, and I don't see this war ever being won. You've been infected with Fidel's fantasy of victory right around the corner—while I don't see that at all. Every day there's more news of slaughters all over the island. Batista's not giving up. Fidel's entire troop could be wiped out. Can't you see that? I'll never understand why you have this notion that victory is imminent. That is delusional. And what really floors me is that now you're a killer."

"A killer? That's how you see it?" I was annoyed.

"I'll never understand the change in you," he said, still not looking me in the eye. He was looking down, his boots stubbing the dirt, and he was talking very deliberately, as if he'd long considered what he wanted to say and finally had the opportunity.

"Just why in hell are you involving yourself to such a lunatic extent in this war?" he said. "It's not your fight. It is not our fight. We came as reporters, remember? That was our plan. What reporting are you doing? None. A few scribbles in your little notebook."

I just listened. This was the Griffin I knew. At least he was talking to me.

"Listen," he went on, "it's not right for either of us to be caught up in the fighting. It simply makes no sense. Do you really think you can make a difference? And now you've put me in a damnable position. Do you think I like being here with people thinking I'm a coward? That I'm dead weight on the great patriotic effort?"

He paused. I said nothing.

"I had no idea you had this degree of credulity. They told me you've been engaged in several skirmishes already, that you've become a revolutionary killer. If that's not true, tell me right now."

I didn't understand his lack of solidarity with the movement, his lack of any fighting spirit. My taking up this fight was not something I could change. I turned away. Further arguing seemed futile.

"Are you even hearing me?" he demanded, gripping my arm, stopping me.

"I'm hearing you, but I don't know what to say. I didn't plan this. It just happened. I know you despise all the injustice we've seen, all the crimes and suffering. I know you do. So explain why you don't hate the army the way I do."

"Because they're simply ignorant," he replied, "Batista's soldiers are stooges. They're misinformed. They don't even know what they're doing."

"All the more reason to stop them from doing it. Yet you excuse them! You call them simple innocents and me a murderer! Unbelievable!" I realized how deeply stung I'd been by his judgment.

"Where do you go when I don't see you for days?" I asked. "You disappear without even letting me know where you're going or what you're doing."

"I'm doing real work," he said. "You're the one that's been going off without a backward glance or a word of explanation. Who the hell knows what you're up to? Do you even know? No! You just take orders. It's like you've caught some revolutionary virus, wanting to please the great man."

The bitter tone of his voice got to me. He must have felt he had gone too far. Despite the hot sting of tears blurring my vision, I could see the emotion in his eyes. We took hold of one another and stayed that way while the surge of pure feeling subsided. Then we stepped apart.

"I guess you're a pacifist," I said, shaking my head. "A conscientious objector."

"Maybe," he acknowledged. "I'm objecting, that's for sure."

We stood in silence for a moment of mutual consternation.

"Listen," he said then, his voice softening, "I probably shouldn't condemn you. I was just shocked by it. I never expected this. All at once you're off somewhere fighting and maybe getting killed or seriously wounded and you never even discussed it with me. Not one word. Know what I'm saying?"

I nodded. The right words weren't arranging themselves for me. I was absorbing how much he seemed to care.

"I don't want to sound like some judgmental jerk," he said. "Can we at least keep talking?"

"Of course," I said with relief. "We're friends. I need our friendship."

"Can you give me a chance to talk you out of more fighting?"

I was considering this when René approached us, urgently summoning me.

"Okay," I said to Griffin, giving his shoulder a gentle cuff. "But not now."

"Not now," he said. "Of course not now. You have to follow orders."

* * *

I was carrying another armload of wood to the cooking shed when I came upon Celia. She was sitting on the ground just outside the shed, smoking, sewing a red and black *26 de Julio* armband onto the arm of a khaki jacket. She appeared to be surprisingly relaxed, even cheerful.

"*Hola,* Paul," she said. "Want to know some good news?"

"*Seguro,*" I said, "What is it?"

"Well," she said, "Fidel has made a strategic arrangement with some ranch owners. They are bringing many cattles into the mountains. The *guajiros* will be taking care of these cattles for us to eat. Soon we'll be eating *bistec* on many days."

13

July, 1958

One evening Fidel called us all together in the dusk. He waited while we got ourselves positioned in a loose cluster among the trees around him. There were nearly thirty of us at that point, smoking cigarettes or cigars or chewing chunks of sugar cane. Dr Vallejo seated himself beside me, translating as well as he could without being disruptive. Fidel began by telling us that M-26's urban underground was succeeding in numerous cities, despite increased violence by the police and the army. He praised Raúl and Ché, saying their front in the Sierra Cristal had success-fullly attacked a number of garrisons capturing supplies and weapons. They had blown up bridges and ambushed troop convoys. He proudly announced that we had finally set up a telephone that linked command posts in the *territorio libre*. He said this was symbolic of the extraordinary progress being made. He particularly praised Juan Almeida and Camillo Cienfuegos for leading import-ant actions in the lowlands.

When Fidel paused briefly, Celia whispered something to him. Right after that Fidel announced that the two *periodistas de Nueva York* were now working with the movement. One was doing educational work with moun-tain children, while the other had become a *combatiente*. A few heads swung around to look at me. Many men nodded acknowledgment. There was no chorus of approval, but I appreciated the quiet sense of acceptance. Fidel then continued his briefing. The doctor whispered to me that Batista's police had recently raided the University of Havana, jailing professors. Batista's forces coming into the mountains were much greater in number, and those forces were being told to assume that all the locals were enemies—including women and children. Gruesome reprisals were being enacted throughout the country. While this was not a new situation, Fidel believed the sheer brutality of it—and he was speaking with great emotion—was increasing mass support for our movement: a critical point was rapidly being reached. He finished by saying that most of Oriente Province was with us, that invaluable support was spreading throughout the island. He said that we were now, each of us, fully imbued with the revolutionary zeal of all the fighters we had lost.

Furthermore, he wanted us to know we would soon be joining forces with Raúl's column to undertake an important mission, We were on our way, he said, to a final series of triumphant missions. We applauded by quietly shaking our fists in the air. I was doing this when I noticed René moving around, speaking quietly to a few people. Word was we were going to attack a garrison. We were leaving immediately.

"*Compañeros y compañeras, Patria es Humanidad*" Fidel summed up. "*Hasta la victoria siempre. Venceremos, Patria o Muerte.*"

I didn't need any translation for that.

"*Patria o Muerte,*" the Doctor and I murmured, as did nearly everyone there. The sun was setting behind a distant ridge of the mountain, turning the shadows deep blue beneath the trees, lighting up hundreds of cobwebs, provoking the frogs in the trees, little green ones that made chirping sounds at sunset or whenever anyone went near them. Merging with the frog calls was the clicking of weapons being loaded. Plates were being scraped clean with leaves. Two rebels went around kicking dirt over the fires. Those who had their weapons apart for cleaning hastily reassembled them. Hammocks and bedrolls were rolled tight. Leather bandoliers of ammunition were slung over shoulders and necks. Handmade rifle grenades were stuck into belts and backpacks. Crude mortars were strapped onto backs. Three of us pulled the camouflaging branches off a jeep parked beside the creek. Calixto and Juan positioned a .45 caliber machinegun in the rear of the vehicle. Preparations were completed within thirty minutes of René's announcement. Three rebels moved slowly around the site with flashlights to ensure nothing had been dropped, forgotten, or left smouldering.

Then René slid behind the steering wheel of the jeep. Fidel climbed in beside him. Calixto and Juan settled themselves behind the machinegun and with a meshing of gears the vehicle lurched into the stream and headed down the canyon. Two rebels splashed along in front of it with flashlights, occasionally calling back warnings of deep holes or boulders, so the headlights wouldn't be needed. Ciro and another rebel led three mules carrying supplies and, I was told, some handmade bombs. The rest of us followed in haphazard single file along the creek bank, sometimes wading in shallow water, stumbling occasionally as darkness increased, but moving rapidly down the mountain. There was no talking. I carried my carbine and a leather satchel containing Dr Vallejo's medical equipment. My synapses were tingling. I felt a deep undeniable joy at being part of this group moving swiftly through dark woods. I wanted to remain perfectly aware of everything, to feel myself in unison with the others. I missed Griffin. Even moving with this dedicated group, I felt an undeniable sting of loneliness. It had been at least a week since I'd talked with him.

The jeep left the creek and passed through a stretch of aromatic flowering trees. The heavily laden mules had to be urged forward. Puddle-pocked and overhung with branches, the trail was barely wide enough to allow passage of the jeep. René was a good driver, advancing at a steady clip for quite some time before coming to a long upward grade. The tires spun furiously in the mud. Each time this happened we set down our gear and pushed until the vehicle achieved sufficient traction to continue. At the top of the grade the trail widened into a muddy dirt road that led across a long field, then downward again. We were now in the foothills. Ahead of me the line of rebels moved ghostlike in and out of shadows, nearly silent but for the low growl of the jeep and the occasional rattle and clink of weapons.

We passed through a small village, then through a field of sugar cane and on through another village. *Campesinos* waved at us from darkened doorways. Many stood along the edge of the road, offering drinks from jugs of water or plastic bottles and quietly calling out wishes for luck and strength. Gradually the sky clouded over, obscuring the stars. A faint smudge of moonglow provided just enough light for me to make out in the mist ahead a large group of men emerging from a dark thicket and melting in among us, probably doubling our number.

The newcomers were led by a wiry figure with a beard, black beret and strikingly commanding air. Breathing heavily, he squeezed into the back seat of the jeep.

"Ché," someone whispered audibly, "*Es* Ché Guevara."

I got only a glimpse of his face. Dr Vallejo had confided that while he had certain reservations about the Argentinian doctor, there was no question at all about his dedication and physical courage. He was deemed exceptionally valuable. Although asthma attacks sometimes hindered him, he was widely admired for struggling even in combat to overcome them, and for his fierce competence in combat. The Doctor told me that some of the *comandantes* considered Ché equal to Fidel in strategic vision.

Maybe a mile farther on we all halted in a clearing where three large flatbed trucks awaited us. On one of them, a machinegun was positioned on a tripod behind a small pile of sandbags. The mules were relieved of their loads and tied to a tree. We began clambering aboard, trying to get situated. I was just climbing on when Dr Vallejo rushed over and retrieved his satchel. Celia was right behind him, holding his sleeve, urging him to get back into the jeep.

"*Buena suerte,*" he said to me, "*hombre, mucho cuidado.*"

"*Igualmente,*" I murmured back.

All three truck motors were revving. After handing my rifle to a dark young woman with freckles and braids, I hoisted myself up to sit beside her. I'd never seen her before. Our legs dangled together near the rear lights. I saw she was missing a front tooth. This provoked a swift impulse to hug her. I didn't. Our rifles were pointed upwards as one by one the big trucks backed out of the clearing and started down the steep road behind the jeep. We were on the middle truck. Soon we were hurtling downhill, barreling over potholes, skidding heavily at turns, caroming off the dirt banks. We were thrown against one another, jarred and bounced around at a rate that made it impossible to think about anything but holding on.

The land began to flatten out, and soon the dirt road became a paved one running in a fairly straight line across the plains. All flashlights were turned off. A few of the men still held lit cigarettes carefully cupped in their hands. The mountain sanctuary fell away behind us. The night air took on a brackish odor suggesting the sea. Miles later we turned off the highway onto a rough gravel road. All talking ceased. All cigarettes were put out. For what seemed a long time, the trucks crawled forward in low gear, gravel crunching, headlights out, until we came to a halt near a stand of palmetto trees beside some railroad tracks. Tall weeds grew between the wooden ties. We helped one another off the trucks. In the distance beyond a field of tall weeds, we could see our target—an army garrison said to be heavily stocked with weapons and housing perhaps a hundred soldiers. A cyclone fence enclosed the large compound, including the field. A cluster of concrete block buildings was illumined by floodlights affixed to stanchions at each corner of the fenced area.

We could see troop carriers, tanks, and an array of other vehicles. Our mission was to disable all vehicles, collect all the weapons and medicine that could be found, and get away without casualties. Juan and Calixto carried the machinegun and tripod through a newly cut gap in the fence and across the field. They were followed by the mortar team. A number of rebels with rifle grenades were spread out facing the main building. René appeared and hurriedly led me and a few others, through the fence, and all the way to several stacks of railroad ties situated near the main entrance to the second largest building. He told me to stay there. I could see most of the others were already in the field, fanning out before dropping into the tall weeds to check their weapons and ensure their sights were correctly focused. Camilo Cienfuegos, readily recognizable in his black cowboy hat, was directing a team already rigging explosives under the vehicles.

In the distance a single car sped by, its engine producing a whirring insect sound. Otherwise there was silence. I felt oddly calm, as though my presence in this situation was inexplicably preordained and unavoidable. My task was simply to cover the main doorway. It was well-lit and painted white. René had been insistent about my maintaining a position behind the stacked railroad ties throughout the attack. The pile smelled of tar. He'd given me three clips of ammunition and told me to use them as sparingly as possible. I was experiencing either an unwarranted sense of competence or a simple rush of adrenaline until I realized there were mosquitos busy all over my face and arms. The air was thick with them. I was brushing them off when gunfire erupted, followed by deafening mortar and grenade explosions that shook the ground. Pre-set bombs exploded under the troop carriers. A mosquito took a dive straight into my right eye, making it burn furiously. A soldier emerged from the door in front of me, shooting a revolver. I fired twice and he pitched to the ground. Two rebels came out behind him carrying a stretcher loaded with weapons. They struggled to climb over the fallen soldier. Other soldiers were running toward the door. I aimed with my left eye, and held the trigger back until the clip was empty. I jammed in another one. A scream of pain somewhere to my right was lost in a series of dull, heavy explosions and the deafening stutter of machinegun bursts.

Splinters and larger shards of tar-covered wood were exploding off the railroad ties right in front of me as I slammed in my last clip and tried to rub that damn mosquito out of my eye with the back of a hand sticky with tar. A cloud of stinging sparks showered over us, provoking outbursts of coughing. Bits of dirt kept hitting my face. Soldiers were shooting from the second floor windows and from the roofs when the girl with braids appeared in the smoke a few feet away. Coughing uncontrollably, she motioned frantically for me to follow her. Together we got through the fence and ran side by side toward the trucks. A palmetto disintegrated in a fiery explosion only twenty feet from us. Then a white shock of blinding pain went through my head.

* * *

When I recovered partial consciousness I was sprawled awkwardly on a truck bed. Dr Vallejo was bending over me,

211

cradling my head. We were bouncing along. The smell of vomit was strong, and I could hear loud moaning over the motor's roar. The sky was pale gray and growing lighter. Weapons were heaped beside me. Two men were being tended by Celia. A rebel with a mangled, bloody knee was being settled near me.

"Can you hear me?" the Doctor asked. I nodded, a movement that sent a rush of electrical pain through my head, blinding me for a moment. When I could see again, the Doctor was holding a bloody cloth in his hand.

"Don't move," he ordered. "You may have a concussion."

"Dizzy," I said.

"Don't talk."

"Blink twice for no. Can you see me?" It was a woman's voice, maybe the one with braids. The Doctor pulled the stopper from a bottle of liquid and began daubing the side of my head.

"Be quiet," he said sternly.

Only the motion of the truck, sending ripples of fierce pain in spasms through my head, kept me awake.

"I don't see any shrapnel," the Doctor said. Someone nearby began to vomit convulsively, sounding as if he were choking to death.

"Two of the rebels carried you back," the Doctor said. "They were right behind you when that grenade went off. Men from Raúl's troop." His mouth kept moving but I couldn't hear. Brief intervals of unconsciousness fitfully came and went.

* * *

I woke up and looked blearily around to find Griffin leaning over me. We were hunkered down in a dense grove of fern trees. The sunlight was strong, although fern branches were providing shade without blocking all the light. The air was moist, unusually fresh. It seemed much too late in the day for me to be sleeping.

"Good to see you, man," I said. "Where are we?"

"You look horrible," he said. "They told me you got hit by a grenade or a mortar. I didn't know if you were dead or alive. I've been worried shitless. You were unconscious for a long time. Dr Vallejo says you have a concussion. How're you feeling?"

"Okay, I guess. Is my ear swollen? It hurts like hell. Where are we?"

"I'm not sure," he said, "Somewhere above Minas del Frío. We're supposed to stay here until the Doctor comes to get you."

"It's good to see you,' I said. "Is that girl all right?"

"Who?"

"That girl I was with."

"What's her name?"

"She had braids."

"You didn't get her name! Shame on you. You hear the Nixon news?"

"Nixon?" I said. "The vice-president?"

"Fidel was talking about it last night. Eisenhower sent Nixon on a tour through South America, an imperial jaunt, supposedly a goodwill tour but the people weren't buying it. Especially the students. Wherever he went, they protested. When he got to Venezuela, to Caracas, students stoned his car. I guess it was pretty wild. Eisenhower had to send in troops. Paul, are you awake?"

"Could you talk in my other ear?" I said.

"Is this better?"

"You mean they're starting a war?" I asked.

"Why do you keep touching your teeth?" Griffin asked. "Be careful with that. You haven't washed your hands."

"Just making sure they're all still there."

"Dr Vallejo is more concerned about the US sending military types to Cambodia or Vietnam. He thinks they're up to no good. Fidel agrees with him."

"Paul," he said, "Keep your hands away from your ear! Don't make me smack you."

He was quiet for a long moment. "You were almost killed," he said. "Yet I'm more concerned about it than you are. What the hell is the matter with you?"

"I told you. I feel the same way the others do," I said, as steadily as I could. "Just being part of this movement, being an active part. There's something sacred about it."

"Wow," he said drily. "*Sacred?*"

'Look," I began again, "do we have to talk about this now?" I could hardly stay awake. "Can't you stop being snide for one second? I'd like us to be together in this, but you just keep holding yourself back, above it all. You don't want to die here. Okay. You think I do? But if I wasn't part of this revolution, I think it would be just another way of being dead."

"Don't get so agitated, Paul. Just breathe. You're wounded. You lost a bucket of blood. Do you understand that? Just breathe in and out. You've taken this stand. I can't pretend to like it. It wasn't our plan at all and it worries the hell out of me, but I just want you to recover."

"I hate your disapproval. Griffin," I said. "Please just accept that I have to do this. Can you do that?" He nodded sadly and squeezed my shoulder. I drifted off then, relieved that he was there beside me.

14

Mid-July, 1958

Three of us were on our way to another location. We were on mules. Ayala Mendoza, Dr Vallejo, and me. Ayala was a dark-skinned, extremely thin woman in her late twenties who had grown up in Oriente. She joined M-26 after losing her lover and their baby to *chikungunya*, a deadly disease spread by mosquitos. There was a profoundly mournful quality about her. She was always quiet and remote. Before she fell ill she worked to coordinate the collecting and transporting of food and other supplies between *guajiros* and rebels. The Doctor said she was truly courageous in all her work with the movement.

I was on a mule because, ever since that blast near my head, I'd been sick. Instead of convalescing I seemed to be getting weaker by the day. Furthermore I had a debilitating diarrhea. It wasn't bad at first, but gradually it worsened to the point where I simply could not keep up, and was useless for combat. I felt chagrin and shame. Over and over throughout that hot, windless afternoon, I slid off the mule, hurriedly crouched behind bushes or trees to relieve myself, then pulled up my trousers and managed to get back on. The worst part was not having any toilet paper or underpants. I'd discarded my old underpants when they fell apart. Since then I'd developed numerous sores on my backside. Some were an inch wide. These sores developed scabs that tore loose whenever I yanked my trousers down, causing blood to trickle down my leg. With my trousers pulled up, the arid heat would soon dry the blood into the fabric, which attached itself to the scabs. This cycle kept repeating—a very humiliating procedure, although Ayala and the Doctor tried to make light of it. They offered me water from their canteens as soon as I'd emptied my own. I used the water to partially clean myself. Then the mule's tongue would lick dry the palm of my hand. At some point late in the day, despite strenuous efforts to stay awake, I dozed off and toppled off the animal. After that, Ayala rode close beside me, doing her best to keep me balanced, although she herself was not well.

We were both left with a *guajiro* family that lived in a cave high on the northern side of Pico Turquino. Dr Vallejo promised he would return as soon as he could obtain penicillin and morphine for me and antibiotics for Ayala. He promised to bring me fresh trousers and underwear. I think he gave us instructions on how to treat our ailments but neither of us could remember what he'd said. Everything seemed shadowy and nebulous those first days in the cave. At some point a wounded young rebel named Enrico was brought in. We were all sprawled close together on the damp stone floor. There was nothing on the walls to support hammocks. All three of us slept poorly and intermittently day and night. One of the *guajiros,* a cheerful older woman, repeatedly awakened us to give us water or a helping of strained *malanga* or rice, sometimes with a splash of goat's milk. The odor of sour milk permeated the close air. Flies swarmed over everything. The *guajiro* family included a mildly demented, toothless old man with a white beard, his overworked wife, and their daughter, a pale teenager with one milky eye. A shaggy gray and white goat was kept tethered to a rock near the entrance. The cave was so crowded that the family slept just outside, if they slept at all. We required frequent attention.

I couldn't stand up without getting nauseous and dizzy, often keeling over in a faint. One of the family, usually the old man, had to assist me in getting outside many times each day. At a short distance from the cave he steadied me while I squatted. The young rebel named Enrico was in even worse condition. We were told they had stashed him in the cave with a plan to move him as soon as possible to a mountain hospital. He had mortar fragments embedded so deeply in his chest that his breathing sounded like coughing. His raucous cough was the most audible sound in the cave, until, after a number of days, it grew louder and more raspy, then simply ceased. The *guajiro* girl shouted for her parents, who came running, but Enrico was gone. The girl and her mother dragged him outside and, lacking a shovel, buried him farther along the ridge beneath a couple of feet of cracked shale. I considered asking for his underpants and trousers but hesitated until it was too late. The old man had argued for storing his body in the small refrigerator in the rear of the cave, which made no sense. Useless without electricity, it was a white-enameled old Kelvinator dented in places and scorched in others. We were told the old man had brought it on a *burro* all the way up from his burnt-out shack in the foothills. It provoked in me a recurrent delusion that it contained a bottle of ice-cold ginger ale. At least twice I crawled toward it, burning with fever, only to have one of the *guajiros* lead me back to my blanket. Each time the exertion sent me into unconsciousness. When I finally came to, I was simultaneously shivering and sweating.

One afternoon I awoke to see the wavering figure of Dr Vallejo kneeling over me, putting an object that looked like a hypodermic needle into a cigar box. His face held a beautiful expression of compassion.

"How do you feel?" he asked. "Still having diarrhea?"

I nodded.

"Better concentrate on hydration," he said. "Finish the broth and I'll take your temperature."

The *guajiro* girl wiped my face with a sour rag. The Doctor kneeled down and placed a thermometer under my tongue.

"We want to get you out of here," he said. "It's too damp, and you should be getting some exercise." His fingers lightly probed around my wound. "Amazing how well your head has healed. I've given you penicillin. It won't help the diarrhea, but it should bring that fever down. If that happens by morning, we'll leave."

I studied his face.

"Don't fidget," he said. "Here, read your mail." He plucked a scrap of paper from his shirt pocket and handed it to me. It was a label torn from a can of pineapple. On the back was scrawled, "How the hell are you pal? R. G." The words blurred. I read it several times.

"There are two packs of cigarettes as well," the Doctor said. "René and Calixto left them for you."

Rising a little, I noticed that no one other than the *campesino* family was in the cave. The Doctor eased me back down.

"Where is everyone?" I asked. "How long have I been here?"

"They left this morning," he murmured, studying the little glass gadget.

"Where is Griffin?" I interrupted.

"He's fine. He's either back at the camp or at Las Chivas. Don't worry about him. He's okay. Just rest."

He put a hand over my eyes. "No talking, no thinking. That shot should be taking effect very soon. We'll talk tomorrow. Now rest." His voice lost its edge and became a soothing drone.

We managed to leave around mid-morning. The old man brought two mules to the cave entrance at dawn and saddled the stronger-looking one while Dr Vallejo prepared the other one. The Doctor and the old man helped hoist me onto one of them. I thanked them and started to offer the old man the cigarette packs, but the Doctor cut me short. We shook hands all around, and he started his mule along the path. Mine obediently followed. We rode through a vast green meadow still sparkling with dew. It was truly refreshing to be outside. A mild sensation of euphoria washed over me. The air felt delicious, the sunlight still cool enough to be a pleasure. Tiny white butterflies flew over the path. High overhead a fledgling hawk swooped in lazy circles. These things seemed very important and somehow profoundly reassuring.

After a while the Doctor turned in his saddle and smiled back at me. "About those cigarettes," he said. "I should explain. The *guajiros* are proud of helping us. Most of them think of themselves as part of the *26 de Julio*. They tend to feel insulted by gratitude or gifts."

I told him I thought I understood. We jogged along at a leisurely pace. The sun climbed higher and eventually grew hot enough to lull me into a daze. When I found myself starting to slide off the saddle, the Doctor steadied me. In the early afternoon we stopped to rest in a grove of wild grapefruit trees. We ate a little cheese and dry bread from his satchel, washing it down with canteen water that tasted of purifying pills. The mules grazed on tufts of lank grass. The grapefruit blossoms gave off an acrid perfume. When we'd finished eating, the Doctor read to me a few poems from a thin book by Juan Ramón Jiménez that he always carried with him. He read the poems in Spanish, then translated. It was peaceful and would have been idyllic if the diarrhea hadn't compelled me to go off by myself a number of times.

Back on our mounts and moving on, we both heard a series of muffled explosions from somewhere far away. "Bombs," he said. "They've been dropping them by the dozen ever since our assault."

"Because of the garrison?"

He coaxed his mule into a faster gait and mine followed. "No, the power station at Bayamo."

"What happened at Bayamo?"

"It's not good to talk about it. You know," he said, "during the war as I recall, the soldiers—"

"World War II?"

"Yes. The soldiers rarely talked about fighting between battles. We argued about baseball or soccer or we talked about food and women but never about fighting. Here the men speak of almost nothing else. It worries me."

"But that's what they're living for," I protested, struggling to stay alert in the torrid heat. "It's their life, I mean, our life. You know what I mean. I doubt if they're interested in much of anything outside the revolution."

"Granted, *muchacho,* but the revolution isn't primarily about fighting," he said with an indignation that startled me. "It's not just a matter of conflict. Fidel doesn't merely want another purge."

The animals were moving along side by side. He was holding my arm loosely, keeping me balanced. As he talked, his grip tightened. "Believe me," he went on, "this revolution isn't about a mere change in government. It's born out of belief that all men have immense possibilities for building and creating. We're rebelling against whatever restricts those possibilities. This isn't just a political coup. Pleased understand that."

I nodded. I was hating the dizziness, the disgusting weakness that was beginning to make a buzzing confusion of his earnest voice.

"That's why Fidel tries to keep the fighting to a minimum," he went on.

The sun was too much for me. I strained to comprehend what he was saying but wave after wave of that dizzying heat pounded down against my head until it blotted out the sound of his voice. I was barely awake when we arrived at the run-down ranch where we were to spend the night.

Two rebels greeted us as we rode up. They helped me dismount, then led the mules away while the Doctor and I were ushered into a modest house by their leader, a great shaggy bear of a man named Camilo Cienfuegos. He and the Doctor seemed very fond of one another. They talked like a couple of life-long pals while the Doctor and I took turns drinking ladles of water.

Then, throwing his tremendous arms around the two of us, Cienfuegos took us on a tour of the place. Formerly a waiter at the Waldorf-Astoria Hotel in New York, he'd agreed some time earlier to let me interview him, and to help if I needed assistance with translating. Behind the house, in a ramshackle building that looked like a deserted barn, we were shown the rebel equivalent of a munitions factory. At least six men were inside, all of them hard at work. Some were using blowtorches to shape thin sheets of steel. Others were measuring out powder allotments. Behind an old-fashioned forge a fire was burning. The heat in the barn was staggering. Looking exactly like a blacksmith, Cienfuegos motioned toward several stacks of mortar shells and rifle grenades piled to an impressive height against one wall.

"Resourceful, no?" the Doctor said with obvious pride. "About a fifth of all the bombs dropped on the Sierra are duds. When we find them, we bring them here, where they're taken apart and made into our kind of weapons."

We were led over to a bomb that must have weighed five-hundred pounds. Soil was still caked around the bright brass on its mashed nose. Tapping it, Cienfuegos looked at me and said something the Doctor didn't translate.

"*No comprendo,*" I said.

"*Defectiva,*" Cienfuegos said, still smiling in a oddly censorious way. "*De los Estados Unidos,*" he persisted,

"Hecha en su patria. This big bastard was made in your country."

* * *

With several others who'd been wounded, I'd been placed by Dr Vallejo in another cave. Uneventful days passed in something of a blur, although one afternoon a violent storm broke directly over us, bringing lightning and thunder for nearly an hour. One horse tore free from its constraints and bolted in panic into the woods.

I was sitting near the cave entrance when the first flight of bright birds suddenly arrived, an astonishment. They vanished just as suddenly in a rush of scattered noise, so many of them—startling, disturbing, off they went careening into the leaves, kicking up bursts of dust and leaf fragments. It was impossible to make out their exact colors, brilliant, tropical, maybe parrots or parakeets, bright flashes in the foliage.

My back was against a tree, rough bark behind my head, legs sprawled out straight in the dust. Impossible to sleep in all that racket. Keeping my eyes closed was important, closed tightly against the heat and dust. I heard a chicken, a thrilling noise like a rooster's, one we might eat in the evening. We might have roast chicken with rice and beans. Celia would know how to kill it. Then came another rush of birds crashing down, making bright flashes above me. Impossible to see clearly. Trying to focus while attempting to suppress my bowels, I felt my left arm being roughly yanked, almost out of its socket. It was Juan standing over me, Juan Almeida, shouting at me, really hurting my arm. I tried to talk but he was angry, very angry. I apologized in Spanish. On top of everything I had to try to speak Spanish. I didn't understand what I said. I wrenched my arm loose and kicked at him, but this only made my bladder release. Hot piss began soaking my trousers, trickling down, making a puddle in the dust, drowning ants in the dirt. Juan jumped back, avoiding a kick, still shouting. Then Griffin was there, Griffin! He was pulling me away from the tree, hands under my shoulders He was dragging me through the piss toward the cave. Juan was trying to help him. Those muscular arms meant business.

Yet another flock came bursting out of the sky, leaping upward the instant they landed, making that sound like slappings, hurried slappings. Maybe they hated the heat. Griffin was leaning in front of me. He looked frantic.

"Paul," he was yelling into my ear, "They're strafing us! Those are bullets! You have to help us get you under cover. God Almighty, can't you understand?"

* * *

By the time the fever had abated sufficiently for me to think with some clarity, I was in a different location. There was the loud braying of a nearby *burro*. I was indoors. Various men around me were smoking and talking quietly. I sat up, aching all over, eyes crusted almost shut. I was lying on a cot on the dirt floor of a hospital-jail *bohio*. Sitting cross-legged a few feet away was a boy concentrating on cleaning a revolver. Next to me was a young army prisoner, watching me over the brim of a glass of coffee.

"*Buenos días*," I said.

"*Buenas*," he drawled, "*¿Quiere usted café?*"

Then Dr Vallejo appeared beside me, looking troubled.

"You had a bad night," he said. "No coffee for you. You were delirious for a number of hours. We have to discuss this. I've spoken with Fidel. He's very concerned."

The prisoner scooted off to the side. The Doctor thanked him and lowered himself to the floor next to me.

"You shouldn't have put me on this cot last night," I told him.

223

"I didn't," he said. "The prisoners did that, *muchacho*. They drew straws. You had a very bad night. You were delirious. Several times you shouted for a girl. Do you remember at all?"

"No," I said.

"You wept, too," he went on. "For a good thirty minutes you sat bolt upright and stared ahead, talking a blue streak."

"What did I say? "

"You were incoherent."

"And I cried?" I said wonderingly. It all seemed unreal, but I had a distinct feeling of shame.

"I suppose it woke everybody," I said miserably.

He was now sitting beside me on the cot. "It looks like you've contracted either bacillary or amoebic dysentery. It hardly matters which."

"You're sure of this?"

"We can't be certain without laboratory facilities, but the likelihood poses a number of problems. Let's hope it's not one of the worst varieties. You've been on antibiotics for days but your strength is not returning."

I was confused. "Didn't we just get here last night?" I asked him.

"You've been here four days," he said. "We need to make a plan, Paul. We have to get you to a hospital."

"A hospital?" I asked in a queer tone. "You mean I have to leave?"

He nodded firmly.

"I'm a liability."

"Paul," he said. "You're seriously ill. You need medical help, and soon. The medicines I've given you aren't working. Your friend Griffin has been notified. He expects to meet us tomorrow at La Plata. That is, if you're strong enough for the trip."

Not trusting my voice, I pulled a burr off my shirt sleeve and slowly crushed it between my fingers.

"I'm sorry," the Doctor said.

I inspected the spikey bits of burr in my palm then took a deep breath. "I can get there," I said. "I'll do whatever you need me to."

He gave my arm a sympathetic squeeze.

"Get yourself washed," he said. "José can give you a hand. He's brought some underwear and trousers for you. I'll have the mules ready this afternoon. We'll leave as soon as it's dark."

Only then did I recognize the boy busily cleaning his revolver as José, our sullen guide when we'd left Bayamo months ago. As soon as the Doctor summoned him, he holstered his weapon and stood up and came over, hand extended, broadly grinning. I was astonished.

15

August, 1958

Fidel made me feel much better about having to leave. He, Celia, Dr Vallejo, René, and Griffin were gathered in the early evening around a table in the largest shack at La Plata. As the Doctor advised, I was sipping at a small bowl of broth while the others enjoyed a meal of roast chicken and yucca with rice. Fidel commented on my weight loss, observing I had lost forty or fifty pounds. René said that at this rate he would soon have to surrender the distinguished name *El Flaco* to me. Then Fidel announced that Griffin and I would soon be leaving. Although I didn't fully understand or can't remember all he said, it sounded like a particularly emotional speech, more than a little hyperbolic, in which he praised each of us, saying that we each embodied the most important quality of a true revolutionary—that it was clearly our natures to feel deeply the injustice suffered by others. He added that either of us or both would be heartily welcomed back to the new revolutionary Cuba that was emerging. Although I was somewhat dizzy, barely able to sit upright, hearing him say this was reassuring. I had every intention of returning, yet was choked up at the thought of leaving, not wanting to, only slowly becoming accustomed to the necessity of doing it simply to stay alive and to not be a burden to the movement. I began wondering how Griffin was responding to Fidel's comments when Fidel unexpectedly pulled off from his own shirt his *26 de Julio* armband and handed it to me. He then embraced me. I had already decided I'd wear that armband with indescribable pride every day the rest of my life. In fact, it was folded under the sock in my left boot the very next day as we rode mules—René, Griffin, and myself, still very shaky and feverish—down steep mountain trails all day until we reached a small farm in the foothills. Celia had given me some pills for diarrhea. They mostly worked, yet I was immensely relieved to discover the house at the ranch had an actual toilet, even though it was outdoors in a tiny shed full of cobwebs.

There was also, as we learned at dawn the following morning, a vintage Ford sedan parked in a small barn behind the house. René appeared with his hair and beard neatly trimmed, wearing the white collar and black suit of a Catholic priest. We laughed of course, yet it was a very impressive get-up. He let us know that, as a teenager, he had earnestly considered becoming a priest. His mother wanted this to happen but his father was a believer in Santería, a Yoruba religion from Africa, and wouldn't permit it. René pointed out that Fidel was risking a great deal by helping us leave the mountains and travel through Cuba. He said that if we were caught by the army or the police we would likely be tortured and would likely disclose important information about the movement—we might tell them who was up in the mountains and where they were, how many they were, and so much more. Very few, René said, were capable of withstanding certain forms of torture. He spoke gravely about the great danger we now faced. He warned us to be constantly alert, and to never in any way do anything that might draw attention to ourselves. I missed the rifle I'd carried for months.

Before noon, with René driving, we reached Manzanillo, a small city on the coast. While I remained dozing in the car, René and Griffin bought new black trousers and white *guayabera* shirts for Griffin and me. We changed into them on the long drive to Camagüey. I was startled by how dark Griffin looked in his new white shirt. With eyes closed I listened to him describing the traffic on the road—most of it military, army personnel trucks, loaded with troops, army flatbeds carrying howitzers, army trucks empty, and many jeeps. We passed a train whose flatbed cars were loaded with tanks. Nearly all the military traffic was heading in the opposite direction, going south, toward the mountains. We passed a motorcyclist who had been pulled over by a police car. They seemed to be checking his papers.

When we finally reached Camagüey, René stopped in the outskirts at a small, dilapidated church. We waited in the car while he went in. A half hour must have passed before he appeared in the doorway and motioned us to join him. The priest at the church, a sad-looking, elderly man with a grey beard, welcomed us politely before hurriedly ushering us through an interior courtyard to a back room where there was a bed and a cot, both neatly made up with clean white sheets and pillows. It had been months since we'd seen anything like that.

That evening René went out and brought back some street food for Griffin and himself, pork sandwiches with ripe tomatoes and bottles of cold Hatuey beer. I understood that they wanted me to continue fasting, just sipping water, but was delighted when René gave me a little white carton filled with a cold white substance he called *helado de chirimoya*. He said it would be good for me. It was the most wonderful thing I'd ever tasted. *Chirimoya* ice cream. Sweet, with a curious flavor all its own. René told me they had probably just scooped the white pulp out of its skin, removed the seeds and chilled it, adding nothing. Still, I could only spoon down about half of it before falling asleep again.

Griffin wanted to go out that evening to explore Camagüey. René explained with exasperation that absolutely no risks were to be taken. In any case a military curfew was in full effect. The police and the army had orders to shoot to kill anyone on the street after dark. The situation on the streets was entirely different than it had been in the spring. He was worried about what might confront us at the airport. He told us that Fidel had made certain arrangements for our departure, but their success was dependent on circumstances beyond his or René's control. I urged him to tell us how we could get a bus to the airport. That way he could avoid the risk of us getting stopped.

"No," he shook his head—Fidel had been insistent that René see us all the way to the airport. I assumed we were fairly close, but in fact we had another three hundred and fifty miles still to go.

The next day we spent on the highway, except for the several times René pulled off the road so I could stumble out and relieve myself, or undergo an attack of dry heaves. I was still extremely ill. Griffin helped me again and again. It was nearly twilight when we pulled into Jagüey Grande, a small town not far from the provincial airport where tickets would be waiting for us, if all went well. René pulled over to the curb to ask directions of a pedestrian, and once again we found ourselves at a small church. The priest at this one was extremely nervous. He didn't even want to shake hands. René's efforts to calm him were useless, but at last he led us to his office, whose bare floor held a desk and a chair. I asked for a glass of water, then stretched out on the floor behind the desk and immediately fell unconscious.

The next day we had to kill time, many hours, waiting for the specific late afternoon plane that had been chosen for our departure. The priest wanted us out of his church early in the morning. René didn't want to risk our possibly being noticed in the airport parking lot or the airport itself. Cautiously choosing the route, he drove around Jagüey

Grande and then out into the local countryside, Griffin in the front seat, me prone in the back. The fever had returned. Sick, and very sick of being sick, I kept quiet, not wanting to be more annoying than necessary. Griffin and René kept talking enthusiastically to one another in Spanish, laughing often. The sound of their voices seemed to come from very far away.

Then it was time. Griffin warned me to stay as alert as possible. He daubed water onto my face from the canteen. He told me I might not be permitted onto the plane if I appeared to be very ill. He told me that René had let him know that a *compañero* from Raúl's front had been shot dead in the Havana airport only three days earlier. There were brief moments when my mind was somewhat clear. During one such memorable moment I asked Griffin how he was feeling about our leaving.

"Mixed responses, I guess," he said. "I fell in love with those *guajiro* kids. I hate leaving them."

"Fidel is going to win," I insisted. "I'm certain of it. That will improve things for those kids and all the other Cubans."

"I've never had your certainty about that," he said. "I don't think he has enough support. Regular Cubans are wary, Catholic, conservative. They're not exactly flocking to Fidel. Anyway, my concern is about getting you to a hospital."

"I can't thank you enough, Griff. I apologize for being so damn weak. I hate it. It's disgusting.You're probably saving my life."

He shrugged it off.

At a few minutes after 5 p.m., we pulled into the airport parking lot. René told us to listen very carefully, then repeat back to him our instructions. As we no longer had wallets or any identification papers, it was essential for us to do this exactly as Fidel (or more likely, Celia) had planned it. He said we were to walk inconspicuously across the lobby directly to the Cubana Airlines kiosk, where a cousin of Haydeé's was expected to have just begun her shift. The clerk would have our tickets and boarding passes. René paused while Griffin repeated the instructions. Once we had secured our tickets and boarding passes, René said, we were to go straight to the gate and board the plane. We were not to go to a restroom or a candy-dispensing machine. We were not to buy a newspaper. As we got out of the car, René discreetly handed each of us a folded US twenty-dollar bill.

"Compañeros, muy buena suerte," he said then, warmly embracing each of us in turn, before he drove away.

Griffin stayed close to me, steadying me through the doors into the airport and toward the Cubana Airlines counter. I stared straight ahead, straining to hold my shoulders back and yet control my breathing. The young clerk had lovely caramel-toned skin and a curiously stern expression. She handed us tickets and boarding passes. Griffin held my arm and leaned close to me as if we were engaged in intense conversation. I concentrated on maintaining an upright posture. It wasn't easy. René had timed it so the plane would be just ready for take-off. Breathing heavily, holding tightly to the railing, I slowly climbed the metal stairs into the plane, with Griffin right behind me. He handed our boarding passes to the stewardess and directed me into a window seat near the front. He took the aisle seat next to me. I leaned back and immediately fell asleep. We were in the air when I awakened to see the ocean extending beneath us.

"Griffin," I muttered. "Will we ever get back into those mountains?"

I guess he didn't hear me. He was busy signaling a flight attendant for a drink.

The End

Afterword

Only a few months later, on January 1st, 1959, dictator Fulgencio Batista fled Cuba, taking with him a substantial portion of the national treasury. His armed forces were in thorough disarray, defeated by the rebels of the 26th of July Movement. All across the island there was rejoicing.

Photographs from the Sierra Maestra

The Author with Fidel Castro in the Sierra Maestra, 1958

Bill McIlver, Fidel Castro & Bob Baldock, Sierra Maestra, 1958

The author in the Sierra Maestra, 1958

The author with Fidel's combat unit, Sierra Maestra, 1958

The author with Fidel (left) & Celia (centre), Sierra Maestra, 1958

The author with René Rodríguez, Sierra Maestra, 1958

Also available from The Clapton Press

FIRING A SHOT FOR FREEDOM: THE MEMOIRS OF FRIDA STEWART with a Foreword and Afterword by Angela Jackson
Frida Stewart drove an ambulance to Murcia in 1937 to help the Spanish Republic and visited the front in Madrid. During the Second World War she was arrested by the Gestapo in Paris and escaped from her internment camp with help from the French Resistance, returning to London where she worked with General de Gaulle. This is her previously unpublished memoir.

BRITISH WOMEN AND THE SPANISH CIVIL WAR by Angela Jackson – 2020 Edition
Angela Jackson's classic examination of the interaction between British women and the war in Spain, through their own oral and written narratives. Revised and updated for this new edition.

BOADILLA by Esmond Romilly
The nephew that Winston Churchill disowned describes his experiences fighting with the International Brigade to defend the Spanish Republic. Written on his honeymoon in France after he eloped with Jessica Mitford.

MY HOUSE IN MALAGA by Sir Peter Chalmers Mitchell
While most ex-pats fled to Gibraltar in 1936, Sir Peter stayed on to protect his house and servants from the rebels. He ended up in prison for sheltering Arthur Koestler from Franco's rabid head of propaganda, who had threatened to 'shoot him like a dog'.

SPANISH PORTRAIT by Elizabeth Lake
A brutally honest, semi-autobiographical novel set in San Sebastián and Madrid between 1934 and 1936, portraying a frantic love affair against a background of confusion and apprehension as Spain drifted inexorably towards civil war.

SOME STILL LIVE by F.G. Tinker Jr.
Frank Tinker was a US pilot who signed up with the Republican forces because he didn't like Mussolini. He was also attracted by the prospect of adventure and a generous pay cheque. This is an account of his experiences in Spain.

Also available from The Clapton Press

NEVER MORE ALIVE:
INSIDE THE SPANISH REPUBLIC
by Kate Mangan with a preface by Paul Preston

When her lover, the German refugee Jan Kurzke, made his way to Spain to join the International Brigade in October 1936, Kate Mangan went after him. She ended up working with Constancia de la Mora in the Republic's Press Office, where she met a host of characters including WH Auden, Stephen Spender, Ernest Hemingway, Robert Capa, Gerda Taro and many more. When Jan was seriously injured she visited him in hospital, helped him across the border to France and left him with friends in Paris so she could return to her job in Valencia.

This first edition includes a Preface by Paul Preston, an Afterword by Kate's daughter, Charlotte Kurzke, and a note on certain key Comintern agents in Spain by Dr Boris Volodarsky.

THE GOOD COMRADE, MEMOIRS OF AN
INTERNATIONAL BRIGADER by Jan Kurzke,
with an Introduction by Richard Baxell

Jan Kurzke was a left-wing artist who fled Nazi Germany in the early 1930s and tramped round the south of Spain, witnessing first-hand the poverty of the rural population, later moving to England where he met Kate Mangan.

When the Spanish civil war broke out in 1936, Jan went back and joined the International Brigade, while Kate followed shortly after, working for the Republican press office. Many of his fellow volunteers died in the savage battles on the outskirts of Madrid and Jan himself was seriously wounded at Boadilla, nearly losing his leg.

This is his memoir, a companion volume to *Never More Alive*.

Also available from The Clapton Press

STRUGGLE FOR THE SPANISH SOUL
& SPAIN IN THE POST-WAR WORLD
by Arturo and Ilsa Barea
with an Introduction by William Chislett

During the Spanish Civil War, Arturo and Ilsa Barea worked for the Republic's Press and Censorship office, operating from the Telefónica building in Madrid. After the civil war they sought refuge in the UK, where Arturo broadcast weekly bulletins to Latin America for the BBC World Service. *Struggle for the Spanish Soul*, an essay on contemporary Spain calling on the democracies of Europe to unseat Franco, was published in 1941. Spain in the post-war world, published in 1945, made similar arguments, which also fell on deaf ears. Together the two essays present a horrific picture of the early years of the dictatorship, which was to endure until Franco's death in 1975.

THE FIGHTER FELL IN LOVE:
A SPANISH CIVIL WAR MEMOIR
by James R Jump
with a Foreword by Paul Preston and a Preface by Jack Jones

Aged twenty-one, James R Jump left his Spanish fiancée in England and went to Spain to join the International Brigade. He was mentioned in despatches for bravery during the Battle of the Ebro. His previously unpublished memoir brings back to life his time in Spain and the tragic course of the war he took part in, while the accompanying poems reflect the intense emotions sparked by his experience.

The Clapton Press